Programming the BBC Micro

John D. Ferguson
John Gordon
Louie Macari
Simon Rushbrook Williams
Anthony Shaw
Peter Williams (Ed.)

GW00674541

Newnes Technical Books

Newnes Technical Books
is an imprint of the Butterworth Group
which has principal offices in
London, Boston, Durban, Singapore, Sydney, Toronto, Wellington

First published 1983

© **Butterworth & Co. (Publishers) Ltd, 1983**
Borough Green, Sevenoaks, Kent, TN15 8PH, England

British Library Cataloguing in Publication Data

Williams, Peter (Editor)
    Programming the BBC Micro
    1. BBC microcomputer (Computer)—Programming
    I. Title
    001.64'2   QA76.8.B/

    ISBN 0-408-01302-8

Typeset by Phoenix Photosetting, Chatham
Printed in England by Butler & Tanner Ltd., Frome and London

Preface

Microcomputers: A perspective

The development of the steam engine can be traced over centuries, the aeroplane over decades. In each case the concepts, in the sense of a vision of their future uses, long preceded the reality. We are living through the development of microcomputers: it is proceeding at such a pace that visions and realities merge and the life-cycle of some machines has been so short that their death is predictable at birth.

This makes it difficult to see any overall pattern. Perhaps we can gain confidence from studying the patterns of these earlier technologies. Man's dream of flight is part of myth and legend; the vision of how it might be achieved emerged, rose and fell with each attempt and each failure—it was desirable, so it must be feasible. Sometimes, as with the balloon, the problem was solved by changing it; man could take to the air without attempting to emulate the flight of the bird.

Eventually the technology caught up with the visions and the first unsteady flights took place. But were the pioneers driven by a vision of the long-term benefits to mankind, the chance of becoming the next generation of millionaires or by inner compulsions that ignored facts when they were inconvenient? Was it desirable and hence inevitably feasible?

Each of these factors played their part in the growth of the industry, with the urgent demands of war triggering off even more rapid changes at intervals. A new factor then seems to emerge. As other related technologies throw up fresh techniques for which there is no immediate use, the imagination of designers is caught and fresh visions are created. Now it is feasible and so must be desirable! This is the period when enthusiasts are swept away by the beauty of the ideas, and particularly where simpler facts are ignored. How long? How much? How many? Who? When? For those with longer memories, names like the Bristol Brabazon may come to mind, but the obvious example is the Concorde. It was feasible so it must be desirable. So much effort was expended on creating and promoting Concorde that what customers were willing to pay for took second place. This demand instead has been met by the tour operators, the Lakers of this world.

Can we deduce anything from this highly selective view? We must first remind ourselves of the compressed nature of the microcomputer's development. Instead of clearly defined stages of a single product, we will find overlapping and interlocking development cycles. Nonetheless, the microprocessor industry has a history deriving from electronics, computing, telecommunications ... There are elements in each of these that are familiar. The dreamers conceived of machines that could not be built by the available technologies; visionaries grasped the implications of each new technological change, anticipated and then shaped it. In the case of computers, their speed, power and range of functions increased to match the demands placed on them. It was and is an uneven process: research and development projects, particularly government sponsored, funded more and more complex systems. These in turn became available to the industrial and commercial world. Many projects in both spheres were over-ambitious and we are all familiar with the computer-gone-berserk. These were the projects which were patently desirable—and therefore assumed to be feasible. It is arguable that only by overreaching can real progress be made. It is true that failed projects can yield results usable in others, but successful ones should yield more.

A further factor in these large projects is the separation of the designer from the user. Perhaps this is inevitable. The design itself is a multi-layer process with system software and hardware considerations interacting. It is part of the success story of the microcomputer that winners can be traced back to individual designers—designers who were looking for solutions to their own problems.

If we combine these features we may see the successes and failures of the microcomputer world differently. Almost anything is feasible. The main-frame computer and the electronics and telecommunications industries provide the reservoir of techniques and skilled practitioners. Almost anything is desirable. The market expands from mere hundreds and thousands of government and industrial customers to the small companies, the teachers and the taught, the hobbyist and the consumer. Within this enormous range any supplier will find some outlet for his product, and, provided the development costs are not too high, can expect a measure of success.

The true mass-market product is different. The first success of the Sinclair ZX81 stems from a brilliant design coupled with aggressive marketing, and a price which places it in the impulse-buying category. This route is perhaps now blocked by the very success of the original and it is in the next price range that the BBC microcomputer is competing. By the nature of its sponsors it must seek to reach the general public. The manufacturers too are geared towards the general rather than a specialist market. It is this involvement with the users of the product that is the key: the BBC microcomputer is a user's machine.

This is a property we might expect of all products, but so often price constraints, the dead hand of 'the committee' or the idiosyncrasies of the designer inhibit it. Over and over in discussion, users and potential buyers voice the same yearnings—for a micro-computer that *does* things. The things vary, but users are tired of having to make or buy extras for sound generation, graphics, laboratory interfacing, serial and parallel outputs. The BBC microcomputer includes the best selection yet of these functions. On the software side, both BASIC and Assembler are automatically present—a feature found on only one or two other machines. Much has been said of the dialect of BASIC. It is not fully structured, but is a considerable improvement on most other BASICs even in this respect. The extensions in BBC BASIC share the philosophy of the hardware extras—they provide useful functions with a directness and simplicity that is admirable. The beginner can bring the machine under control with a very limited vocabulary and the minimum of external units to connect. At last the desirable and the feasible are merging.

We would like to thank John Coll of Acorn Computers Ltd, Bob Salkeld of the BBC, and their colleagues for advice and assistance.

Thanks are also due to Henry Budgett, Editor of *Computing Today*, for the loan of the machine for the cover photograph.

P.W.

Contents

1
Introduction

The BBC microcomputer is different. Some of the differences are apparent, others hidden. It still owes its development to ideas from earlier machines and it is interesting to observe such similarities as it is looked at more closely. (We will refer to the machine as a micro since microcomputer is a bit of a mouthful—and wastes space!)

A detailed specification is given in Appendix A but certain points stand out. The appearance (*Fig. 1.1*) is attractive, more so than for

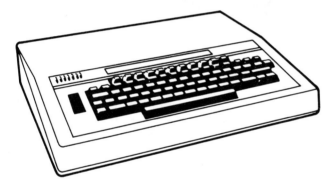

Fig. 1.1. The BBC micro

its (remote) ancestor, the Acorn Atom. The construction is simple and economical, with a two-part case of lightweight plastic and a single large printed circuit board. The only reservation is that the structure with its large flat surface tempts the user to put the monitor/TV receiver on top—and this is expressly forbidden by the manufacturers. It will lead to trouble because even with the monitor placed behind the micro, there is every likelihood of it being propped up on the back lip to get a better viewing angle. No doubt enterprising manufacturers or users will produce sturdy bridges across the micro to take the load.

1

Fig. 1.2 shows a well laid out keyboard with 'extras'. Before turning to the keyboard proper, two obvious and useful items can be noted:

the small loudspeaker under the slots at the left of the transparent strip above the keyboard,
the rectangular slot to the left of the keys which will house optional ROM-packs for future expansion.

Fig. 1.2. The keyboard

The most striking feature of the keyboard itself is the set of ten red function keys labelled fØ to f9. They can be programmed to hold functions, commands and even short programs that can be recalled by pressing the appropriate key—their detailed use is explained later. The transparent strip can be unclipped to insert labels when the keys' functions are fixed by the user.

So far there is no indication of any differences between models. The manufacturers have announced two versions, Models A and B, with identical keyboards and basic functions. In fact to upgrade from A to B needs only the addition of the appropriate chips and input–output sockets. These sockets can be seen at the rear of the micro and are shown in *Fig. 1.3*.

All that is needed to get started is a mains plug and a domestic TV set with cable linking it to the socket marked UHF at the back of the micro. The transformer and regulator are self-contained in a metal case inside the micro and become distinctly warm after a few hours use.

Plug the BBC micro into the mains, connect the UHF output to the receiver aerial socket—or from the BNC socket providing a video output to a video monitor—or from the RGB (red/green/blue)

2

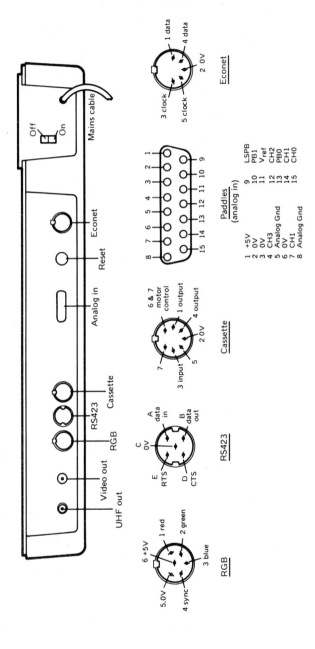

Fig. 1.3. Input/output sockets. Those fitted on Model B are indicated separately, the others are fitted on both

3

output to a suitable colour monitor. In the first case, either a black-and-white or colour television can be used—an adjustment to the capacitor controlling the colour burst generator proved necessary on some prototypes but should not be a problem with production versions. The receiver should be tuned to channel 36 and the message BBC Computer 16K (or 32K for a Model B) should be obtainable with the prompt > indicating that it is ready for a command or line number. Tuning is not necessary with a video monitor.

The ESCAPE key, top left, interrupts any BASIC program and prompts with a screen message identifying the particular line number at which it was interrupted: it will not interrupt a program running machine-code routines.

Pressing the BREAK key at the top right-hand side of the keyboard takes the micro out of any closed loop it might be in, initiating a so-called 'warm' start with the message

> BBC Computer
> BASIC
> >

Note the absence of the memory size information: if by accident or design the BREAK key is pressed twice in quick succession, the original cold-start message is obtained and any commands stored via the function keys, but *not* normal programs, are lost.

More information on peripherals and dealing with faults is postponed till later.

Description of functions

The keyboard in *Fig. 1.2* reveals a conventional QWERTY or typewriter layout with some useful extras. The keyboard is of good quality and is liked by beginners and experts (though the latter will never be completely satisfied). A light touch is sufficient and should make for good speed with practice. If a key is held down its function is repeated until released. This is particularly useful with the editing keys—the four arrows (top right) that move the flashing cursor anywhere on the screen, and the DELETE and COPY keys (bottom right). The DELETE key moves the cursor back one position at a time, deleting characters as it goes; a complete line can be deleted in a second or so. The COPY key provides a novel alternative to the usual editing methods. Instead of modifying an existing line, a new one is created by copying any section or sections of lines displayed on the screen, adding new characters from the keyboard as needed.

4

This may sound odd at first, but it is a real boon with mathematical functions or those where spelling or punctuation is important. It is so easy when retyping a line to correct one error and introduce two more!

The procedure is simple. As soon as the cursor arrows are used, a flashing underlining bar responds leaving a white square at the current active point on the screen unaffected by the cursor arrows. The flashing line is then moved under the first character to be copied and the copy key drives it to the right—the right-pointing cursor key is used to skip over unwanted characters. The characters are copied into the original active line at the foot of the display, the white square moving accordingly. Sections of any other lines displayed on the screen can be added regardless of whether they were program lines, text or direct commands. Any doubts about the effectiveness of the method are removed by typing in a few lines of program or even random characters and experimenting. It soon becomes second nature.

At the left hand side of the keyboard the CAPS LOCK key gives upper case on the letters. SHIFT or SHIFT LOCK selects the upper characters on all the keys. The LEDs indicate their current status and also the remote control status for an external cassette recorder: trial and error will quickly give the feel for these keys in a way no amount of explanation can.

Hidden under the micro are slots giving access to sets of contacts on the edge of the printed-circuit board. They are mainly for future expansion to disc, network and external microprocessor systems. In the long term they could become the most important feature of the system, with the original micro acting as an intelligent full-colour graphics terminal to a much larger computing system. With the rapid changes in competition in this industry, it is hard to know whether something is a miracle or a mirage.

Programming in practice

A car is useless without a driver and so is a computer without a program. A bad driver can break a car but a poor program will not damage a computer. However, an excellent program and a poor computer will yield no useful work; neither will an excellent computer and a poor program. The computer today represents one of the great triumphs of science and technology but it is of no use if it doesn't have a program. The program should be treated with all the care and attention with which the results it produces will be.

Unfortunately, despite our claim to logic, we as animals tend to jump to conclusions by complex thought processes. The computer does not, and needs to be instructed step by step what to do. As an example look at the following list of numbers and pick out the largest.

$$1, 5, 2, 7, 2, 6, 10, 22, 6, 10$$

Try explaining how you reached the conclusion that 22 was the biggest. Until this is understood it is impossible to write a program to get a computer to find the largest number. You probably started with the left-hand side of the list and picked 1 and then compared it with the next number on the right which was 5, and asked the question 'Is one greater than five?' The answer is no, and so forget one and remember five. Now compare five with the next number. 'Is five greater than two?' The answer is yes, so move to the next number. Carry on with this until the end of the list and you will remember the largest number. This verbal description of how to find the largest number from a list of numbers is a program. It is a logical sequence of operations which will achieve the desired end product.

Unfortunately, a computer doesn't (yet) understand speech or English as a language, and so as well as giving a logical sequence of instructions you must give the sequence in instructions understood by the machine. These instructions are called the program language and for most of this book the program language is in a form of BASIC called BBC BASIC.

BASIC consists of a series of valid commands. Once the BBC is switched on it will announce itself either as a 16K (model A) or 32K (model B) machine. Finally it will print an > which is called a 'prompt'.

Type PRINT "HELLO" and then press the RETURN key. If all is well the machine will print HELLO on the screen and give another prompt. If a mistake was made then it will report this. The word PRINT must be in capitals and there must be two sets of "s.

Type PRINT 2+2 followed by the RETURN key and the machine will answer 4. Now type PRINT "2+2" and this time 2+2 will be printed.

A PRINT statement causes the machine to output onto the screen either the result of a calculation or exactly what is within quote marks.

Now try X=2+2, followed of course by the RETURN key. Nothing happens. Actually the machine has worked out 2+2 and has stored it away in a location called X, but as it was not asked to print it, it didn't. So now type PRINT X and the answer 4 will result.

Try A$="HELLO" then PRINT A$ with the RETURN key

being pressed between each command. The $ sign signifies a word not a number.

The screen will look a little untidy now so type CLS for 'clear screen' and the screen will blank with the arrow prompt at the top left-hand corner of the screen.

The commands we have used so far have been executed by the computer immediately the RETURN key was pressed; these are referred to as 'immediate commands'. It is usual, however, to write a string of commands and execute them later. To do this we need to both write the commands and tell the computer the order in which we wish to do them. Type 10 PRINT "HELLO" and RETURN. Note that nothing happened. Now type RUN followed by RETURN and the computer will print HELLO. By adding a line number the instruction was no longer treated as an immediate command but as a program line. The number ten could have been any number; as we only have one line it can only be executed in one order. If we add another line with a number less than ten, then this line will be executed first and if we add a line with a number greater than ten it will be executed after the PRINT command.

Type 20 GOTO 10. This is a command that tells the computer to go back to line ten. Type RUN again and the screen will fill with HELLOs very quickly. To stop operation, as the program is in an endless loop, press the ESCAPE key at the top left of the keyboard.

To view the program just written, type the command LIST and a listing of the two lines will appear.

An extra line can be added by simply typing 15 PRINT "FRED" and LIST again. Notice how the line has been inserted in the right place. If you wish to change a line, simply retype it. To erase a line, type the line number and then the RETURN key.

There are times when the whole program needs to be erased. In this case type NEW and now a LIST will produce nothing. However, if you type OLD then LIST the program returns. This acts as a one-stage safety net. It is also a way to recover a program after the BREAK key has been pressed.

RENUMBER is a feature which allows the programs to be renumbered. RENUMBER or REN on its own will renumber starting at ten in steps of ten. If this is unsuitable, then RENUMBER first number, interval, will control the process. So RENUMBER 1, 1 will start at one and number in steps of 1. RENUMBER 100,500 will start at 100 and number in steps of 500. It should be noted that not only the line numbers are altered by also all the GOTOs, etc., in the program.

DELETE allows blocks of lines to be erased, so DELETE 20,40 will erase all lines between *and including* 20 and 40.

For the lazy there is also an AUTO feature. When typed the computer will insert line numbers for you, in order to save typing them. To stop the AUTO feature, the ESCAPE key needs to be pressed.

Another feature of the machine is the list/option command LISTO n, where n is a number from zero to seven. (Note that the computer distinguishes between O and zero.) The list option inserts spaces and indents loops to make the programs more readable. Experience has shown some problems in screen editing using the cursor controls and the COPY key if the list option is greater than 1 as extra spaces get inserted.

The LIST command itself is complex in that LIST 40,100 will list all lines between 40 and 100 and LIST, 100 will list all lines up to 100. Obviously LIST 200, will list the rest of the program from 200 onwards.

The BBC BASIC has many features which make the machine easy to program. The programs in this book illustrate many of these features and are written in a way which best emphasises them. However, much experience is gained by typing in simple programs to examine certain features.

Consider the following lines:

```
10 PRINT "HELLO";"FRED"
20 PRINT "HELLO":PRINT "FRED"
30 PRINT "HELLO"
40 PRINT "FRED"
```

RUN this program to look at the use of colons and semi-colons.

The random number generator can also be looked at as follows: type 10 PRINT RND(10) and RUN this program a few times. Every time it is RUN, a different number between 1 and 10 is printed.

It is always worth exploring a new command by a little program rather than using it in a complex one when its action may not be clear.

SAVE and LOAD allow you to save a program to tape or disc while LOAD gets it back. In order to distinguish between programs, they each have a name. Before typing in a long program, check that the SAVE and LOAD commands work.

While copying and running the programs in this book is well worthwhile, writing a program for yourself is far more enjoyable and convincing that the commands are understood. Creation of an original program involves three stages.

These three steps, termed:

(a) design
(b) implementation
(c) testing,

are used to create all programs. Often, however, they are badly defined and the result is programs that don't work properly. Everyone has their own stories of computers that 'go wrong' when they mean that the programmer made a mistake.

The most difficult step is the first, program design. This cannot be done if you don't understand the problem or how to solve it. Once done the computer will solve problems more rapidly and with greater precision. Design skills cannot be taught, they have to be acquired. Certain rules apply but for the most part the better the problem is understood, the easier the design.

A program should be an object of beauty, with as much design, care and efficiency as the circuit board of the microcomputer. If it is thrown together in any old fashion with no regard for error checking and completeness, then it will probably work in any old fashion. Programs are creations and most of computing is work in the creation of better programs.

With experience, a little care, and a logical mind anyone can become a good programmer.

2
Practice in programming

Solving a problem using a computer

There are three 'proverbs' which must be borne in mind when approaching a computer to solve a problem:

1. Never attempt to solve a difficult problem when a simple one will do.

2. If a program can go wrong, it will.

and thirdly

3. The sooner you start to code, the sooner you generate errors.

Chapter 3 covers the various aspects of error handling using the BBC micro.

However, let us consider the first proverb—never attempt a difficult problem when a simple one will do. What does this mean— surely if we have a difficult problem then that is what we have to solve? The answer to this question is no!

Every problem which is solvable by computer has some kind of structure; it is made up of subproblems. It is the task of the problem solver to think about the structure of his problem, to see whether it can be broken down into a series of subproblems, each of which, hopefully will be simpler to solve. Consider an example: suppose we have the following problem:

'Write a computer program to solve any quadratic equation'

A programmer would not normally just go ahead and code a program to solve this problem, but would first of all consider the problem in its entirety. In other words he would write a more detailed specification. Perhaps he would end up with:

'a quadratic equation is an equation of the form
$$ax^2+bx+c=0$$
where a, b and c are parameters and x is the unknown.

The solution to this equation is given by the formula
$$x = (-b \pm SQR\ (b^2 - 4ac))/2/a$$
Note that this formula breaks down in the following cases

$a = 0$ we have a division by zero if we use the formula, but in this case solution is given by
$$x = -c/b$$
If b is also 0, then we do not have a problem to solve.

$b^2 - 4ac < 0$ In this case we would attempt to find the square root of a negative number, which cannot be done for real numbers.
Here we have to introduce complex numbers solution
$$x_1 = -b/2/a + i*SQR(4ac - b^2)/2/a$$
$$x_2 = -b/2/a - i*SQR(4ac - b^2)/2/a$$
where $i = \sqrt{-1}$ and will be printed onto the screen.

Write a computer program, which will accept in three parameters via the keyboard, solve the corresponding quadratic equation, and write the answer.'

Once the detailed specification has been decided, the programmer can break it down into a series of subproblems, in this case the result would be *Fig. 2.1*.

The programmer can now code each part of the problem without too much difficulty. Notice that the problem breakdown pointed out the case $b^2 - 4ac = 0$, which was not considered in the specification.

Functions

As well as the standard mathematical functions such as $SIN(X)$ or $COS(X)$ the BBC micro allows you to define your own functions. Suppose the area of a circle needs to be worked out at various places within the program. It would be possible to code the calculation $A = \pi R^2$ wherever it is needed, but a better approach would be to define a function. This is done as follows:

    100 DEF FNarea(R) = PI*R*R

where PI is replaced by its value of $= 3.14159265$.
DEF is short for DEFINE and is the keyword in this statement.
FNarea is the name of the function. In BBC BASIC, all functions

begin with FN, and a meaningful name can then be tagged on. *Fig. 2.2* gives examples of function declarations.

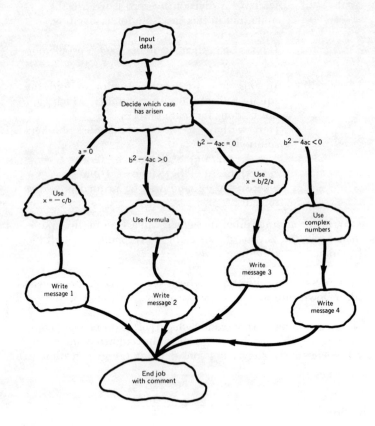

Fig. 2.1. Problem structure—quadratic equation

```
200 DEF FNquadratic(X) = 3*X*X + 2*X + 14
210 DEF FNdirac(X) = X*SGN (1+ SGN(X) )
220 DEF FNinterest(years) = princ*(1+annual_rate/100)*years - princ
```

Fig. 2.2. Function declarations

12

Functions can then be called as if they were supplied with the system.

Try out the program in *Fig. 2.3*.

Example

```
100 REM:    This program accepts a radius input to it
            and then calculates the area of the circle.
110 INPUT radius
120 area = FNarea (radius)
130 Print area
144 END
150 DEF FNarea (R) = PI*R*R
```

Fig. 2.3.

Notice in the above program that the data name 'radius' is different from the data name 'R' used in the function definition. When the function is called these two names are equated as if a LET statement had been used:

LET R=radius

before the function is evaluated. The assignment in line 120, then, returns the area of the circle and places this value in 'Area'.

In this example the data name 'R' is known as the argument of the function. In BBC BASIC functions do not have to have a single argument, a function can have no arguments or many arguments. *Fig. 2.4* and *2.5* give examples.

```
100 DEF FNsilly = 3*10 + A*2
110 A = 4
120 PRINT FNsilly
130 END
```

Fig. 2.4.

```
100 REM      This program solves a quadratic equation.
             N.B. Make sure that roots are real.
110 INPUT P1, P2, P3
120 ROOT_1 = FN_root_1 (P1,P2,P3)
130 ROOT_2 = FN_root_2 (P1,P2,P3)
140 PRINT "Solution is X=   "Root_1" or "Root_2"
150 END
160 DEF FN_root_1 (A,B,C) = (-B+SQR(B*B-4*A*C))/2/A
170 DEF FN_root_2 (A,B,C) = (-B-SQR(B*B-4*A*C))/2/A
```

Fig. 2.5.

Notice that in *Fig. 2.5* the function:

SQR (B*B−4*A*C)

13

is evaluated twice, this could have been declared as a further function.

```
160 DEF FN_root_1 (A,B,C) = (-B+ FNdeterminant(A,B,C))/2/A
170 DEF FN_root_2 (A,B,C) = (-B-FNdeterminant (A,B,C))/2/A
180 DEF FNdeterminant (A,B,C) = SQR (B*B-4*A*C)
```

Fig. 2.6.

Let us consider the structure of the function declaration:

DEF FN-name = Computed Value

We can see that it has four main parts. In BBC BASIC, the user defined function can be far more flexible than most other BASIC, in that the function declaration can extend over many lines. *Fig. 2.7* demonstrates this.

```
100 REM : this program exhibits a multiline function
110 INPUT A,B
120 Result = FNMultiline (A,B)
130 PRINT Result
140 END
150 DEF  FNMultiline(X1, X2)
160 Mean = (X1 + X2)/2
170 D1 = Mean - X1 : D2 = Mean - X2
180 Deviation = SQR (D1*D1 + D2*D2)
190  =  Deviation
```

Fig. 2.7.

Notice that we still have the four main parts but now we have subsidiary calculations between the function declaration and the = sign. We could, however, introduce problems with this approach. Notice that in line 160 the variable 'Mean' takes a new value, as does 'Deviation' in line 180. Now, suppose that you have already used these names elsewhere in the program, then calling the function FNMultiline will change their values. This is not a very satisfactory state of affairs.

Fortunately, BBC BASIC can get round this problem by allowing us to declare such variables as being LOCAL to the function. Thus we can add the following lines.

155   LOCAL Mean, D1, D2, Deviation

To see the effect of this line, we add in the following lines of code:

105   Mean=5
135   PRINT "Mean=", Mean

14

If we then run the program, inputting A=10, B=20 then the output is

7.07106781
Mean=5

The value of 'Mean' remains unchanged. If on the other hand line 155 is deleted, then output would be

7.07106781
Mean=15

Thus we see that the value of 'Mean' has been changed by executing the function.

As well as being able to call other functions, BBC BASIC allows functions to call themselves. This feature is known as *recursion* and can be an extremely useful technique.

Example

The mathematical definition of factorial is

$$N! = \begin{cases} 1 & \text{if } N<2 \\ N.(N-1)!, & \text{otherwise} \end{cases}$$

where N is an integer. In BBC BASIC, this is coded as in *Fig. 2.8.*

```
100 REM : program to calculate factorial N
110 INPUT N%
120 PRINT  FN_factorial (N%)
130 END
140 DEF FN_factorial (N%)
150 IF N<2  THEN  = 1
            ELSE  = FN_factorial (N-1)*N
```

Fig. 2.8.

Subroutines

A more traditional method of collecting a set of lines together is to use subroutines. If, within a program, a programmer finds that he has to repeat a section of code many times, then he can collect that section of code as a subroutine.

The programmer transfers control to and from the subroutine by using GOSUB . . . RETURN.

Example
Suppose we have the program in *Fig. 2.9.*

15

```
100 REM : a silly program to show the use of subroutines
110 INPUT A
120 B = 3*A + 49
130 PRINT B
140 A = A + 4
150 B = 3*A + 49
160 PRINT B
170 A = A + 6
180 B = 3*A + 49
190 PRINT B
200 END
```

Fig. 2.9.

Notice in this program that two lines of code

B=3*A+49 and PRINT B

are repeated three times.

Another way of writing this piece of code would be as *Fig. 2.10.*

```
100     REM: a silly program to show the use of subroutines
110     INPUT A
120     GOSUB 1000
130     A = A+4
140     GOSUB 1000
150     A = A + 6
160     GOSUB 1000
170     END
1000    B = 3*A + 49
1010    PRINT B
1020    RETURN
```

Fig. 2.10.

Notice the format of lines 140 and 1020. In line 140, we transfer control to line 1020; the machine at this time will record where it is transferring from. In line 1020, we return to where we transferred from.

Program control then flows in the following fashion:

Line Nos: $100 \rightarrow 110 \rightarrow 120 \rightarrow 1000 \rightarrow 1010 \rightarrow 1020 \rightarrow 130 \rightarrow 140 \rightarrow 1000$
etc.

In BBC BASIC, and in other forms of BASIC, there is no way of making variables local to a subroutine. Thus it is good programming practice to include REMARK statements detailing what variables are used in the subroutine (see *Fig. 2.11*).

```
1000    REM : this is the silly subroutine used in the
                silly program.
1010    REM Subroutine inputs  :  A
1020    REM Subroutine output  :  B
1030    REM Other variables used : none
1040    B = 3*A + 49
1050    PRINT B
1060    RETURN
```

Fig. 2.11.

16

In this particular example, it might seem that the routine is over-weighted with REMARKs, but in more realistic examples these will become very necessary.

One further use of subroutines is when we need to make a complex decision. Suppose we wish to execute one of three subroutines depending on an input to the program in *Fig. 2.12.*

Example

```
100   REM  :  this program shows the use of multiway switch
                           using IF Statements
110   CLS
120   PRINT''"Computer Assisted Learning - Lesson 1"
130   PRINT ''"Select option required by inputting the
                appropriate number".
140   PRINT ''"1.  Geography of Paisley"
150   PRINT ''"2.  Industry of Paisley"
160   PRINT ''"3.  Culture of Paisley"
170   INPUT N
180   IF N = 1 THEN GOSUB 1000
190   IF N = 2 THEN GOSUB 2000
200   IF N = 3 THEN GOSUB 3000
210   REM  :  the rest of the program follows
500   END
```

Fig. 2.12.

In this example, after N is input, control will be transferred to subroutines at 1000, 2000 or 3000 depending on the value of N. Eventually control will pass on to line 210. Notice that no subroutines will be executed if N has a value other than 1, 2, 3.

A better way of coding this program is to use the ON . . . GOSUB construct. To do this we delete line 180, 190 and 200 and insert the following:

180   ON N GOSUB 1000, 2000, 3000

The two versions of the program are then equivalent. The format of the ON . . . GOSUB is as follows.

ON variable GOSUB Line 1, line 2, line 3 . . . .

If 'variable' =1   GOSUB line 1 is executed
          =2   GOSUB line 2 is executed
          =3   GOSUB line 3 is executed
          etc.

If the variable is not one of the above values, or if there are not enough subroutines in the list, then control will pass on to the next statement.

BBC BASIC allows us to collect all invalid responses to the ON . . . GOSUB, to allow us to catch errors.

In the program we would replace the new line 180 by:

180   ON N GOSUB 1000, 2000, 3000: ELSE PRINT "NOT IN RANGE"

Thus if N does not have the values 1, 2, or 3, the message NOT IN RANGE will be printed.

Procedures

To get round some of the problems of subroutines, it is possible in BBC BASIC to declare a Procedure and to pass parameters to this procedure. This allows the programmer to work large programs in the form of a series of smaller procedures—the so called 'cornerstone of programming'. These procedures can then be later combined to form the full program. If the procedures could also be recorded separately in a 'library' then the language could be effectively extended. In Chapter 3 we consider how to do this using the cassette and disc systems.

The procedures available in BBC BASIC are well designed and easy to use, as demonstrated in *Fig. 2.13*.

```
1000 DEF PROCprocedure-name : REM all procedure names begin with
                              PROC
1010 REM This procedure only prints a message, normally
         procedures would be more useful
1020 PRINT "This is a silly procedure"
1030 ENDPROC : REM procedure declarations end with ENDPROC
```

Fig. 2.13.

To call this procedure we simply state its name following the PROC statement. For example, the following line calls the procedure 'procedure–name' which has been defined as above.

100   PROCprocedure–name

The above procedure could be considered as equivalent to GOSUB in traditional BASIC except that the subroutine name can mean something to the user rather than just a line number.

BBC BASIC has other useful features. For example variables can be declared as LOCAL to the procedure, as in *Fig. 2.14*.

In this program, Index takes the values 1 to 10 within the procedure PROCjimmy but maintains its value of 100 in the main part of the program. Furthermore, BBC BASIC allows values to be passed to parameters that are used within procedures where such parameters will be local to the procedure. This is accomplished by incorporating a parameter list in the procedure declaration

18

```
>LIST

   10   Index = 100
   20   PROCjimmy
   30   PRINT "Index = "Index
   40   END
  100   DEF PROCjimmy
  110   LOCAL Index
  120   FOR Index = 1 TO 10
  130   PRINT "How's it gawin Jimmy!!!"
  140   NEXT Index
  150   ENDPROC

>RUN

  How's it gawin Jimmy!!!
  How's it gawin Jimmy!!!
  How's it gawin Jimmy!!!
  How's it gawin Jimmy!!!
  How's it gawin Jimmy!!!
  How's it gawin Jimmy!!!
  How's it gawin Jimmy!!!
  How's it gawin Jimmy!!!
  How's it gawin Jimmy!!!
  How's it gawin Jimmy!!!
  Index =        100
```

Fig. 2.14.

DEF   PROCname (parameter-1, parameter-2 . . .)

and a set of values in the procedure call

PROCname (Value-1, Value-2 . . .)

where Value-1 etc. can be literal values or variables which have values already assigned to them.

```
>LIST

  100   REM Main Program
  110   INPUT "Enter three numbers",A,B,C
  120   PROCminimum (A,B,C)
  130   PRINT "Result =" ; Result
  140   END
 1000   DEF PROCminimum (First, Second, Third)
 1010   IF First <Second THEN Result = First
                         ELSE Result = Second
 1015
 1020   IF Third <Result THEN Result = Third
 1030   ENDPROC

>RUN

  Enter three numbers? 5,6,7
  Result = 5
```

Fig. 2.15.

19

In the program in *Fig. 2.15,* when the procedures are called, FIRST, SECOND and THIRD are given their values. If we had used these names somewhere else in the program, the procedure would not have changed their values elsewhere. The only variables which are changed in the main program are those such as Result—that is GLOBAL variables. Any variables not declared as LOCAL or not named in the procedure heading are GLOBAL (see *Fig. 2.16*).

```
100   REM  Main program
105   Result = -999
106   PRINT "Result = "; Result
110   INPUT  "Enter three numbers",A,B,C
120   PROCminimum (A,B,C)
130   PRINT "Result = "; Result
140   END
1000  DEF  PROCminimum (First, Second, Third)
1010  IF First <Second THEN Result = First
                       ELSE Result = Second
1015
1020  IF Third <Result THEN Result = Third
1030  ENDPROC
>RUN

Result = -999
Enter three numbers? 1,2,3
Result = 1
```

Fig. 2.16.

Notice in *Fig. 2.16* the values of Result.

As with functions, procedures can call themselves recursively, as in the following examples.

Example 1. Towers of Hanoi Problem

'In the great temple of Benares beneath the dome which marks the centre of the world, rests a brass plate in which are fixed three diamond needles, each a cubit high and as thick as the body of a bee. On one of these needles, at the creation, God placed sixty-four discs of pure gold, the largest disc resting on the brass plate and the others getting smaller and smaller up to the top one. This is the Tower of Brahma. Day and night, unceasingly, the priests transfer the discs from one diamond needle to another, according to the fixed and irrefutable laws of Brahma, which require that the priest must not move more than one disc at a time and that he must place this disc on a needle so that there is no smaller disc below it. When the sixty-four discs shall have been thus transferred from the needle on which, at the creation, God placed them, to one of the other needles, tower, temple and Brahmas alike will crumble into dust, and with a thunderclap, the world will vanish.'

The above statement of the Towers of Hanoi problem is quoted from Kasno, *Mathematics and the Imagination*, New York, 1967.

The program in *Fig. 2.17* uses a recursive procedure call to solve this problem. We leave it as an exercise to the reader to amend the program to calculate how long it would take the priests to complete their task, assuming that they make no mistakes and that a transfer will take one second.

```
100  REM  :  This program uses recursion to solve the
             Towers of Hanoi problem.
110  REM  :  The program can be amended to simulate
             different numbers of discs, N
120  N = 10  :  REM change this line for different
                numbers of discs.
125  PRINT' "Disc Moved", "Sending Pile", "Receiving Pile"
130  PROCtowers (N,1,2,3)
140  END
150  DEF PROCtowers (N,X,Y,Z)
160  IF  N = 0 END PROC
170  PROCtowers (N-1 X,Z,Y)
180  PRINT  N,X,Y
190  PROCtowers (N-2,Z,Y,X)
200  ENDPROC
```

Fig. 2.17.

3
Program development

Introduction

In this chapter we see how we can build up a library of procedures which can help us to develop programs. One of the biggest problems facing any programmer is error handling. In this chapter we discuss how the BBC micro can be used to handle errors. The next section then discusses keyboard input and how to trap input errors—the so-called GOTCHAS.

One of the more useful features of the BBC micro is the soft keys, which can be programmed by the user to batch up commands.

Program development and program libraries

In Chapter 2 we saw how the BBC micro could be used to build a program in the form of a set of procedures—the 'cornerstone of programming'. In this chapter we see how the BBC machine can be used to build a library of such procedures on disc or on tape. Since most users will be using the cassette operating system, the examples here are based on tape.

Before going into the actual mechanism of our method of library building, there are some technical details which have to be mentioned. If you wish to take our method on trust, then simply pass on to the technique.

Technical details

In the BBC micro different sections of memory are used for different purposes. For example, the text of a BASIC program is stored starting at memory location 3328 upwards. The end of the program is known as TOP. TOP is also a BASIC *function* which returns the address of the first free memory location after the BASIC program.

The BASIC interpreter normally stores the values of data names after TOP. The *variable* LOMEM gives the address of the place in memory above which the BBC micro stores the values of data names. Thus, because LOMEM is a variable, it is possible to change its value under program control, e.g.

LOMEM=LOMEM+&7B

This instruction increases the value of LOMEM by the hexadecimal number 7B.

Also in our procedure we use the instruction *LOAD; this allows us to load text anywhere in memory, e.g.

*LOAD "PROC 1"OE8A

loads the procedure PROC 1 into memory starting at OE8A.

One further point of explanation; the last two locations of a BASIC program contain an end of program marker. Thus to append a procedure onto a program we have to:

1. Find LOMEM.
2. Subtract 2 from LOMEM.
3. *LOAD our procedure into memory starting at LOMEM-2.
4. Increase the value of LOMEM by the length of our program. (The loading procedure gives the length of the program.)
5. LIST to see the result. This also updates the value held by TOP.

Using this technique we can build a library of subroutines which can be patched together to form programs.

There still, of course, remains the problem of line number clashes. This can be overcome by making all procedures on tape start with line number 10 000, say, and RENUMBERing each time a procedure is *LOADED. The following technique allows a series of procedures or subroutines held on tape to be loaded into a contiguous area of program memory. To use this technique the programmer must ensure that the line numbers of all stored procedures or subroutines are in a distinct high range (e.g. 10 000 onwards) with the main program line numbers in a low range, 0–9 000, say. The technique is:

Type in or load the main program in the normal way

Decrease LOMEM by 2.   >LOMEM=LOMEM-2

Examine the value of LOMEM in hex.   >PRINT ᵀᴹLOMEM

Once this new value of LOMEM is known the location in memory into which the procedure is to be loaded can be supplied>*LOAD "PROC1" xxxx (xxxx is the hex. value of LOMEM)

The micro displays a message that includes
the byte length (zzzz) of the program. PROC1 yy zzzz
Increment the value of LOMEM by the byte
count value. >LOMEM=LOMEM+&zzzz
List the program. (This updates the value of
TOP) >LIST
RENUMBER the entire program to ensure
that there will be no line number conflict
when the next procedure is loaded using the
same technique. >RENUMBER

Using this technique a library of procedures, subroutines and functions can be built up and later linked together as required. In order
to be able to use these procedures they must, of course, be properly
documented. The user of the procedure must know all GLOBAL
names and what parameters are passed to the procedure.

Error handling with the BBC micro

There are, broadly speaking, three types of error which can occur in
computer programming:

Syntax errors arise through the programmer using the wrong
syntax, keying in the program incorrectly, and so on.
   The BASIC interpreter catches syntax errors and returns a
message to the programmer (see Appendix B, for a list of BBC
error messages). The programmer thus, after a few attempts,
can ensure that there are no syntax errors in his program.

Logic errors arise through errors in the program design. For
example, if a programmer wanted a program to solve a
quadratic equation, the result could be the set of code in *Fig.
3.1*.

```
200 D  =  B*B-4*A*C
210 IF D=0 THEN 400
220 R1 = -B+SQR(D)/2*A
230 R2 = -B-SQR(D)/2*A
      .
      .
      .
400 PRINT "EQUAL ROOTS"
```

Fig. 3.1.

In this program there are no syntax errors, and when the program was run there would be no errors generated, but still the

24

program would not give out the correct results. Lines 220 and 230 should be:

220 R1=(−B+SQR(D))/2/A
230 R2=(−B−SQR(D))/2/A

The only way to check out your program is to try it out with test data where you know what the results should be.

Run time errors occur when, for example, you have instructed the machine to divide by zero, or calculate the square root of a negative number, etc.

Unlike most machines where the program usually aborts on an error, the BBC micro allows the programmer to take control of the system. This can be done by using the following functions:

ERL: error line number. This function returns the line number of the line where the last error occurred.
e.g. 1000 X=ERL
1010 PRINT "ERROR OCCURRED ON" X

ERR: error. This function returns the error number (see Appendix B) of the last error which occurred.
e.g. 1000 IF ERR=18 THEN PRINT "DO NOT DIVIDE BY ZERO, DUMMY!!"

ON ERROR GOTO)
ON ERROR OFF)

: These two statements allow the programmer to take control of all errors which occur between the two statements. For example see *Fig. 3.2.*

```
100 ON ERROR GOTO 1000
110 INPUT "DIVISOR" ; D
120 K = 100/D
130 PRINT K
140 ON ERROR OFF
150 END
1000 IF ERR=18 THEN PRINT "DO NOT DIVIDE BY ZERO, DUMMY!!"
1010 GOTO 110
```

Fig. 3.2.

REPORT: this prints the error message appropriate to the last error condition.
e.g. 1000 REPORT
1010 IF ERR=18 THEN PRINT "DO NOT DIVIDE BY ZERO, DUMMY!!"

It can be seen, therefore, that the BBC micro provides the programmer with a great scope for error-trapping. If you ever try to write

25

commercial software for the BBC micro, you will have to use these features of the software. This is because of the old adage: 'If it can go wrong, it will.'

Input from the BBC micro keyboard—and gotchas

One of the major advantages of using a microcomputer is that data can be entered to the program while the program is running. In traditional data processing, input to a program is normally from a backing storage device such as cards or magnetic tape (see Chapter 11). Microcomputers, however, are designed so that data can be entered via the keyboard. This introduces a problem to the software designer, who has to ensure that the data entered is valid, in order to avoid 'program crash'. Solutions to this problem are known as 'GOTCHAS'.

However, let us consider keyboard entry as implemented within BBC BASIC. The simplest method of keyboard entry is to use the INPUT statement, which allows the user to input strings of characters or values of parameters to the program.

Example

   100 INPUT parameter

When this statement is executed a question mark appears on the screen, and the computer waits until a numeric value is entered followed by RETURN. As with most other BASICs the INPUT statement can print a message on the screen before waiting for reply.

Example

   110   INPUT "What is the number", number

This appears on the screen as:

  What is the number?

If you do not wish the question mark to appear, then omit the comma.

Example

   120   INPUT "Enter a number and press RETURN" number

When this version is executed the following appears on the screen:

  Enter a number and press RETURN

We can similarly enter string variables (see Chapter 5), the input statement can ask for a series of data entries, thus:

130 INPUT "What is your name", N$, "and your age", age

when this statement is executed, the message

What is your name?.

appears on the screen. When the user replies with his name, the message

and your age?

appears on the next line.

In some of the older BASICs, when the user pressed RETURN without first entering the required data, the program crashed. This involved the programmer in writing code to catch this type of error. On the BBC machine, the null response is valid, thus:

140 INPUT "What is your name", N$, "and your age", age
150 PRINT N$, age

If you RUN this section of code, line 150 prints the following on the screen

0

That is; space followed by zero. Thus if space or zero is not a valid response, we can program a GOTCHA as in *Fig. 3.3*.

```
130 REPEAT: gotcha=0
140    INPUT "What is your name",n$,"and your age",age
150    IF n$="" THEN PRINT "you have entered a null name":gotcha=1
160    IF age=0 THEN PRINT " you have entered a zero age":gotcha=1
170 UNTIL gotcha=0
```

Fig. 3.3.

Another deficiency in traditional BASIC is that it is almost impossible to input a comma as a valid character. This is because the comma is used as a field separator. BBC BASIC allows the user to input a line consisting of any characters to the computer.

Example

100 INPUT LINE N$

This places every character up to RETURN into the string N$.

So far all the data being input to the computer had to be 'RETURNED' to the system. The software designer also wants the capability of single keystroke response, perhaps by giving the user a menu to select from. If the software designer needs such a feature, then with BBC BASIC, he has the choice of four functions.

GET

When this function is executed, the computer waits for a key to be pressed on the keyboard, and then returns the ASCII representation (see chapter on Assembly codes) of the key pressed.

Example

```
100 PRINT "Press any key to continue"

110 anykey = GET
```
Fig. 3.4.

In *Fig. 3.4* line 110 just breaks the flow of the program and as soon as any key is pressed, program extension will continue.

GET$

This is similar to the GET function in that it waits until a key is pressed, but in this case the string representation is returned.

Example

```
100 REPEAT

110 PRINT "Do you wish to continue? (Y/N)"

120 ans$ = GET$

130 UNTIL ans$ = "Y" OR ans$ = "y"
```
Fig. 3.5.

In *Fig. 3.5* the loop 100–130 will be continually executed until the Y key is pressed.

INKEY

This function allows the designer to control the keyboard input. When the function is executed, the computer waits for a specified time (in centiseconds), scanning the keyboard. If no key is pressed when the time is up, -1 (false) is returned and program execution continues. The INKEY function returns the ASCII value of the key pressed.

Example

```
100 PRINT "You have 55/100 of a second to hit a key!!"
110 key_pressed = INKEY (55)
120 IF key_pressed = -1 THEN PRINT "SLOW!!"
```
Fig. 3.6.

The routine in *Fig. 3.6* can easily be amended to write a reaction test program. This is left to the reader as an exercise.

INKEY$

This is similar to the INKEY function but it now returns the character representation of the key.

Example

```
100 ans$ = INKEY$ (100)
```
Fig. 3.7.

The line of code in *Fig. 3.7* waits for 1 second and if no key is pressed, the null string is returned.

Using the above features the BBC programmer has the ability to construct interactive programs fairly easily.

Soft keys

At the top of the keyboard are ten red user-defined keys, f0–f9. They exemplify the thinking behind this design: to hand over more control of the micro to the user. Few other machines have such keys and with ten of them, small groups of quite different functions can be available simultaneously. They are also called *function keys* and *soft keys,* i.e. they can be programmed.

Programming the soft keys

Each key accesses the text stored in a reserved area of memory, sharing between them one page or 256 bytes. Each byte can store a single character and so, allowing for spaces and partitioning, about 20 or so characters should be available per key. There appears to be little if any restriction on the division of this memory, and individual keys

29

may call up longer text if required. Included in this text can be any of the BASIC commands, with the addition of control codes to insert, for example, RETURNs after each command. Thus if the character string corresponding to LIST followed by RETURN is stored under key 5, then at any stage when the keyboard is being scanned, a single keystroke will list the current program. By extension, list options can be set and a printer activated. If these strings could be added only from the keyboard, they would still be very useful for functions required frequently. It is also possible, though, to enter them directly from a program and the first example could be inserted into such a program. On running that program the character string in the quotes would be stored in the section of memory called up by pressing key 5.

10 *KEY 5 "OLD ||M LIST ||M"

On any future occasion that key 5 is operated, say after use of the BREAK key, the old program is recalled and automatically listed with the display showing

>OLD
>LIST
  Line 1
  Line 2
  .
  .
  .

Storing text

One restriction and one warning should be noted. Any material normally enclosed in quotes such as a PRINT "TEXT" sequence will lead to an error message. In common with other BASICs, this is handled by enclosing the text in double sets of quotes—the system is then arranged to interpret them correctly as a single set.

Example

  *KEY 4 "OLD ||M PRINT ""TEXT"" ||M"

would provide the following response on pressing the key:

>OLD
>PRINT "TEXT"
  TEXT
  .
  .
  .

The warning is the obvious but easy to overlook: don't make the character strings too long or the soft key buffer will overflow.

Programming the keys: an example

To get used to the soft keys either load them with some of your own options or try out the program in *Fig. 3.8.*

```
 10 *KEY 0 "OLD IM LISTO0 IM"
 20 *KEY 1 "OLD IM LISTO7 IM LIST IM"
 30 *KEY 2 "VDU 14 IM"
 40 *KEY 3 "VDU 15 IM"
 50 *KEY 4 "MODE 4 IM VDU 26 IM"
 60 *KEY 5 "MODE 5 IM VDU 26 IM"
 70 *KEY 6 "MODE 7 IM VDU 26 IM"
 80 *KEY 7 "MODE 4 IM VDU 28,0,15,39,0IM VDU 24 ,0;0;1279;511; IM"
 90 *KEY 8 "MODE 4 IM VDU 28,0,31,19,0IM VDU 24,639;0;1279;1023; IM"
100 *KEY 9 "OLD IM REN.IM LIST IM"
```

Fig. 3.8.

Check it carefully before running it, particularly to see that the opening and closing quotes are present. Note also that LISTO7 must always be followed by LIST, otherwise nothing happens. Each command stored within the text is terminated with a pair of characters equivalent to pressing the RETURN key. (Depending on the MODE in which the micro was last used, the first of these characters will appear as

‖ MODE 7
¦ MODE 4
| OUTPUT ON SOME PRINTERS).

Run the program. The > prompt should be obtained and the individual keys can then be tested. Remember that they are labelled as f0–f9 on the keys themselves, and are referred to as USER-DEFINED FUNCTION KEYS in the Users' Guide but are often called SOFT KEYS elsewhere. In programming the keys, the words KEY 0 to KEY 9 are used and it is this form that is used in this section. Try pressing them in numerical order and note the results.

KEY 0 The words OLD LISTO0 are displayed and the listing option has been set so that on listing any future program, the automatic indenting of loops is suppressed. Programmers often prefer this so that they can keep to their personal style of formatting. The previous program is recovered by use of OLD and this key is a convenient means of restarting after pressing the BREAK key—either by accident or to get out of a machine code program.

KEY 1 Similarly recovers the program but sets the list options and performs the actual listing. Any FOR...NEXT and REPEAT...UNTIL loops are then indented for ease of reading and a space is inserted between each line number and line.

KEY 2 Gets the response VDU 14 and selects a scrolling mode helpful with long programs. A page is scrolled at a time and the display then halts until the SHIFT key is pressed to resume scrolling.

KEY 3 Restores the continuous scrolling condition, i.e. to its normal state when the machine is first switched on.

KEY 4 Selects MODE 4, clearing the screen in the process and, via the VDU 26 command, resets the graphics and text to their normal conditions of occupying the whole screen independently. MODE 4 has 320×256 graphics resolution with two-colour display, and with 32 lines of 40 characters for the text. The various special characters correspond to those on the keyboard. No actual listing takes place though this command could be added to any or all of the keys if required provided the total text stored does not exceed the 256 byte buffer.

KEY 5 Performs the same function for MODE 5 with its 160×256, four-colour display and 20×32 text.

KEY 6 Similarly selects another text format: the normal or teletext format of MODE 7. This is the condition at switch-on—a confusing choice since the teletext versions of special characters are quite different from those on the keyboard.

e.g.	MODE 4, 5, 6 KEYBOARD	MODE 7 TELETEXT
	~	÷
	∧	↑
	[	←
	]	→
	¦	‖
	{	¼
	}	¾
	\	½

Try out the effects on program listing of KEYS 4–6. Press each key in turn followed by KEY 1 in each case and compare the listings.

KEY 7 This selects MODE 4 and divides the screen into separate areas for text and graphics using VDU 28. The details are covered in the graphics section but the effect is to allot the width of the screen (0–39) between lines 0 and 15 to text. Similarly the lower half of the screen is assigned to graphics by the VDU 24 command. To test this press KEY 7 followed by KEY 1. Press KEY 1 two or three times and the text should scroll only in the top half of the screen. Any graphics, no matter what coordinates, will only be visible for the graphics area—for X=0 to 1279, Y=0 to 511.

KEY 8 This performs a similar function but reserving the left-hand half of the screen for text and the right for graphics. N.B. This separation is not essential and the areas can overlap to any desired extent. Again listing a program will cause scrolling only within the defined text area with lines being automatically reformatted to fit the restricted area.

KEY 9 A minor variant that includes renumbering along with program recovering and listing.

As well as storing and saving these functions using BASIC, it is also possible to store the appropriate page of memory which contains the values representing the individual letters of the files. Using a cassette recorder the procedure would be:

>* SAVE "KEYS" 0B00 0BFF for storing the settings, and
* LOAD "KEYS" 0B00 for retrieving it.

Note

An unannounced extra is that the BREAK key can also be programmed to provide additional functions as KEY 10, so entering
   *KEY10 "OLD ||M LIST ||M"
will cause the original program to be recovered and listed after pressing the BREAK key. A small trick to confuse unwelcome key-pushers is to program the BREAK key instead with OLD and RUN so that it appears to fail in its intended purpose of interrupting a program. The program does stop, but then restarts again almost instantaneously with the 'BBC BASIC' message flashing on the screen for a brief instant.

4
Graphics

Graphics allows the programmer to create graphs, pictures and results in colour and to move them around the screen. Even animation is possible. But first let us look at the screen and some simple commands.

To use the graphics we need to be in a graphics mode. The MODE statement is used to put the microcomputer into one of eight graphics or text modes. These are called MODE 0 to MODE 7. When MODE is executed the text and graphics screens are cleared and the colours set to the default colours with a foreground colour of white and a background colour of black. On model A machines MODES 4, 5, 6 and 7 are allowed with all modes allowed on model B machines. The modes are listed in Table 4.1.

Table 4.1

Mode	Graphics	Text	Colours
0	640×256	80×32	2
1	320×256	40×32	4
2	160×256	20×32	16
3	—	80×25	2
4	320×256	40×32	2
5	160×256	20×32	4
6	—	40×25	2
7	—	40×25	* Teletext display

MODES 3, 6 and 7 are text only modes, though 'chunky' pictures can be made up out of graphics characters in mode 7. In all modes apart from mode 7 the text characters can be altered by the user.

While a display mode might have only two colours these can be any two colours, although after execution of a MODE command they will default to black and white. We will see later on how default colours can be changed. On power up or after a BREAK the micro will be in mode 7, and so before we can draw any shapes we need a line in the program such as 10 MODE 5. It is impossible to change modes and not destroy a picture.

Now let us look at the two simple commands DRAW and MOVE. Each of these is followed by two numbers separated by a comma which represent the 'X' and 'Y' values of the movement. Scientifically it is normal to call movement up and down a 'Y axis movement' and movement right to left or left to right an 'X axis movement'. It is a very useful habit to get into so we will use it throughout this chapter. The X-axis (right to left or horizontal axis) of the screen is divided into 1280 units; the X value of the left-hand side of the screen is zero while the right-hand side of the screen has an X value of 1279. If we start at zero and count up to 1279 we have 1280 units.

The Y-axis (up and down or vertical axis) of the screen is divided into 1024 units; the bottom of the screen has a Y value of zero and the top of the screen has a value 1023, again one less than the axis length.

We have divided the screen into 1280 blocks in the horizontal or X direction and 1024 blocks in the vertical or Y direction; the point where X and Y are both zero is called the 'origin' and is in the bottom left-hand corner of the screen. The top right-hand corner of the screen has an X value of 1279 and a Y value of 1023. *Fig. 6.1* shows the screen and important 'points' on it labelled as X, Y. This is the way used here so a point 102,59 is a point 102 units along the X axis from the origin and 59 units up the Y axis from the origin.

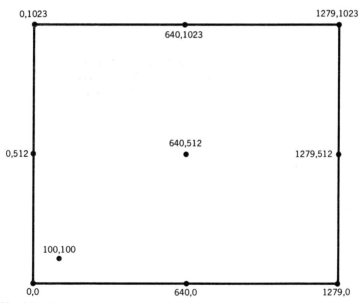

Fig. 4.1. Important 'points' on the screen

MOVE is a command which moves the computer's 'pen' to a given point. DRAW moves the computer's pen to the given point but with the pen drawing on the screen. So MOVE 0,0 moves the pen to the origin where X=0 and Y=0. DRAW 500,500 will then draw a line from 0,0 to 500,500. Write and execute the program of *Fig. 4.2*. Does it do what you expect? It is worth checking these in trial programs if in doubt, to gain confidence for the later sections.

```
 5 REM THIS DRAWS LINES
10 MODE 4
20 MOVE 0,0
30 DRAW 1000,1000
40 DRAW 1000,0
50 MOVE 0,500
60 DRAW 200,500
```

Fig. 4.2.

The program in *Fig. 4.3* will draw a line around the screen. It is important to remember that this program works in any of the graphics modes. The resolution does not matter, well not for a bit anyway.

```
 5 REM THIS DRAWS A FRAME
10 MODE 4
20 MOVE 0,0
30 DRAW 1279,0
40 DRAW 1279,1023
50 DRAW 0,1023
60 DRAW 0,0
```

Fig. 4.3.

Take a close look at the program of *Fig. 4.4*. We are drawing a lot of frames but note how we are reducing the length of the X and Y frame each time. Experiment with this program until you are familiar with X and Y values.

```
100 REM THIS DRAWS MULTIPLE FRAMES
110 X=1279:Y=1023
120 OX=0:OY=0
130 MODE 4
140 REPEAT
150    PROCdrawframe
160    X=X-20:Y=Y-20
170    OX=OX+20:OY=OY+20
180    UNTIL Y<=OY
190 END
200 DEFPROCdrawframe
210    MOVE OX,OY
220    DRAW X,OY
230    DRAW X,Y
240    DRAW OX,Y
250    DRAW OX,OY
260 ENDPROC
```

Fig. 4.4.

MOVE and DRAW are special examples of PLOT commands. In particular PLOT 4, X, Y is identical to MOVE X, Y and PLOT 5, X, Y is identical to DRAW X, Y. The separate names for commonly used commands make graphics easy to start with, but now we are going to look at the plot commands in detail and see what power they give us. A list of eight PLOT commands is given in *Fig. 4.5*. We will look at these in turn.

0	move relative to last point
1	draw line relative in the current graphics foreground colour
2	draw line relative in logical inverse colour
3	draw line relative in current graphics background colour
4	move to absolute position
5	draw line absolute in the current graphics foreground colour
6	draw line absolute in logical inverse colour
7	draw line absolute in current graphics background colour

Fig. 4.5. Plot commands

PLOT 0,X,Y is a move without drawing on the screen but this is a *relative command*. That is, the X value is added to the current X value and the Y value is added to the current Y value. The X and Y values in the plot command are treated as signed numbers so a MOVE 100,100 followed by a PLOT 0,–10,200 would result in a move to 100–10 or 90 in the X DIRECTION and 100+20 or 120 in the Y DIRECTION.

PLOT 1,X,Y is similar to PLOT 0 but a line is drawn in the current foreground colour. The program in *Fig. 4.6* uses this relative command to 'scribble' on the screen.

```
5 REM THIS DRAWS A RANDOM LINE
10 MODE 4
20 MOVE 512,512
30 X=RND(50)-25:Y=RND(50)-25
40 PLOT 1,X,Y
50 GOTO30
```

Fig. 4.6.

The PLOT 2 command will become more obvious when we look at colour but basically if the background is white the line will be black and if black the line will be white. Yellow is the inverse of red and red the inverse of yellow. These will be looked at later but if you feel like experimenting change the PLOT 1 command in the last program and see if you understand what it does.

PLOT 3 is useful for erasing a line that has just been drawn. By drawing in current background colour it blends into the background. Again this is a relative command so the X and Y values are treated as signed values to be added to the current X and Y position.

The next four commands repeat the previous functions, but are absolute commands. That is the X and Y values define the absolute position with 0,0 at the bottom left and 1280,1024 at the top right of the screen. If you use negative numbers here they will be plotted to the left and below your TV screen and you will not see them.

It is worth drawing to your attention that plotting of lines and points beyond the view of the screen is possible even if it seems a waste of time. However, some microcomputers will, if you try this, either signal an error or can 'crash' completely. The BBC micro just obeys your command, even if you cannot see it. So if you write a program that seems all right, but with no visible response, you just might be plotting X and Y values off the screen.

All the plot commands so far defined by the manufacturers, namely 0–31, 6–71 and 80–87, follow the same pattern as described above. Plots 8–15 are identical to the above but the last point is not plotted. To answer the question 'What use is that?', consider a line that has been drawn in red to which a yellow line is to be joined. If you simply draw the line then the last point will over-write the red with a yellow dot. The plot commands of 8–15 will not. To check this, write and run the program of *Fig. 4.7*. A colour TV will help, but with contrast not too high the effect should be clear on a black and white TV. Do not worry about the GCOL command. We will deal with it shortly.

```
 5 REM TWO LINES INTERSECTING
10 MODE 5
20 MOVE 1000,0
30 DRAW 1000,1000
40 GCOL 0,2
50 MOVE 0,500
60 PLOT 13,1000,500
```

Fig. 4.7.

PLOTS 16–23 and 24–31 repeat the function of 0–7 and 8–15 respectively but provide dotted lines. If you want you can draw your own dotted lines alternating DRAW and MOVE commands, but computers are designed to make life easy.

PLOTS 64–71 echo PLOTS 0–7 but with only the last point plotted. Confused? Well, try the program of *Fig. 4.8* and all should become clear. Pay attention to program *Fig. 4.9* which moves a dot around. Animation is very easy with a little effort.

Now PLOTS 80–87 are powerful and we will look at these. They draw a solid triangle in the current graphics foreground colour, the three points of the triangle being the three most recently visited points. Look at the program of *Fig. 4.10* and the results. If this is not

38

obvious try it yourself on the computer and change the X and Y values.

```
  5 REM THIS PLOTS A LOT OF DOTS
 10 MODE 4
 20 FOR X=0 TO 1279 STEP 20
 30   FOR Y=0 TO 1024 STEP 20
 40     PLOT 69,X,Y
 50   NEXT Y
 60 NEXT X
```

Fig. 4.8.

```
100 REM A DOT THAT WALKS AT RANDOM
110 MODE 4
120 X=500:Y=500
130 MOVE X,Y
140 deltax=RND(10)-5
150 deltay=RND(10)-5
160 X=X+deltax
170 Y=Y+deltay
180 PLOT 69,X,Y
190 PLOT 71,X-deltax,Y-deltay
200 GOTO 140
```

Fig. 4.9.

```
  5 REM FILL A TRIANGLE
 10 MODE 4
 20 MOVE 0,0
 30 MOVE 1000,1000
 40 PLOT 85,1000,0
```

Fig. 4.10.

But triangles are a start to many geometric shapes. Blocks can be drawn easily using two triangles, as shown in *Fig. 4.11*. The program is structured to form a procedure which we can use where we want and it seems logical to call it 'drawblock'.

```
100 REM DRAW RANDOM BLOCKS
110 MODE 4
120 X=RND(1279):Y=RND(1024)
130 width=RND(250)
140 height=RND(150)
150 PROCdrawblock
160 GOTO 120
170 DEFPROCdrawblock
180   MOVE X,Y
190   MOVE X+width,Y
200   PLOT 85,X,Y+height
210   PLOT 85,X+width,Y+height
220 ENDPROC
```

Fig. 4.11.

Circles are simply lots of small triangles swept around a centre.

To summarise so far: the MOVE and DRAW commands used at the start of this chapter are special cases of the general PLOT

39

K,X,Y command. K can take many values, and the K results in many different actions. These are grouped in eights with each group of eight having the same basic relative action but a different result on the screen. It is to be hoped that future expansion keeps this format.

Now we come to colour. For those with a colour TV or monitor then this will all make sense. For those without colour some of the effects will be lost. However, as a rule red looks black, yellow looks grey and white and black look white and black. The cyans, blues and greens also look grey and the shades depend on how you have set the contrast and brightness controls on your set. With a little effort you can get a fair grey scale. From now on it will be assumed you have colour.

The initial 'logical colours' before we start changing them (see the end of this chapter) are as defined in *Fig. 4.12*. Note that colour numbers less than 128 specify foreground colours and numbers greater than 128 specify background colours. The usual background is black corresponding to 128, but do not feel constrained to this. If you wish to specify both foreground and background as yellow, then while all your programs will work you will not be too impressed with the results.

4 COLOUR MODE

NUMBER	COLOUR	INVERSE
0	Black	White
1	Red	Yellow
2	Yellow	Red
3	White	Black

16 COLOUR MODE

NUMBER	COLOUR	INVERSE
0	Black	Flashing White-Black
1	Red	Flashing Cyan-Red
2	Green	Flashing Magenta-Green
3	Yellow	Flashing Blue-Yellow
4	Blue	Flashing Yellow-Blue
5	Magenta	Flashing Green-Magenta
6	Cyan	Flashing Red-Cyan
7	White	Flashing Black-White
8	Flashing Black-White	White
9	Flashing Red-Cyan	Cyan
10	Flashing Green-Magenta	Magenta
11	Flashing Yellow-Blue	Blue
12	Flashing Blue-Yellow	Yellow
13	Flashing Magenta-Green	Green
14	Flashing Cyan-Red	Red
15	Flashing White-Black	Black

Fig. 4.12. Logical colours

Text and graphics have different commands to set colour. Text is easy, it is the COLOUR command. So COLOUR 2 in mode 1 or 5 will make foreground yellow and COLOUR 129 in the same mode will make the text background red. We will see the effect of text and graphics with different backgrounds later. Mode 2, if you have a B machine, gives you sixteen colours—eight of which are flashing colours.

Graphics colour is specified with the GCOL command but with one addition. The form is: GCOL logic, colour. The colour is the same as the COLOUR command for text but the logic is a little more complicated.

The logic variable is one of 0 to 4. 0 means the colour is plotted as specified so GCOL 0,2 will plot all following graphics foreground in yellow, while GCOL 0,129 will plot all graphics backgrounds in red. This is the normal GCOL logical number. The next four logical numbers OR, AND, EXCLUSIVE-OR and logical INVERT the colours already there respectively.

Logical colours are not easy unless you understand the logic of OR and AND. To get a feel for these, a bit of experimenting is always useful. These commands allow some very pretty 'trick' programs to be written and shapes or text to be moved in front of or behind other shapes. There is no room in this chapter for a detailed discussion but *Fig. 4.13* shows a program using logical inverse of colour.

```
  5 REM DRAW A LINE IN INVERSE COLOUR
100 MODE 5
110 colour=0
120 FOR X=0 TO 1279 STEP 150
130    PROCdrawblock
140    colour=colour+1
150    GCOL 0,colour
160    NEXT X
170 GCOL 4,3
180 MOVE 0,500
190 DRAW 1279,500
200 END
210 DEFPROCdrawblock
220   MOVE X,0:MOVE X+100,0
230   PLOT 85,X,1000:PLOT 85,X+100,1000
240 ENDPROC
```

Fig. 4.13.

While Acorn have only defined the logical numbers 0–4, we have found that other values have very odd effects and in particular if you PLOT blocks of colour using the PLOT 85 commands then stripes and 'noisy' stripes are possible. Explore these when you feel confident.

Try the random triangle program of *Fig. 4.14* with different colours, backgrounds and plotting logic. We do not guarantee you will understand, but it is different. It demonstrates just what can be achieved with very few lines of program.

```
5 REM RANDOM COLOURED TRIANGLES
10 MODE 5
20 X=1279:Y=1024
30 GCOL RND(15),RND(4)
40 MOVE RND(X),RND(Y)
50 MOVE RND(X),RND(Y)
60 PLOT 85,RND(X),RND(Y)
70 GOTO 30
```

Fig. 4.14.

Run the random histogram program in *Fig. 4.15*. This program should give you ideas if you are in the business of showing data graphically.

```
5 REM RANDOM HISTOGRAMS
100 MODE 5
110 X=0:width=30
120 REPEAT
130   X=X+60
140   Y=RND(1020)
150   GCOL 0,RND(4)-1
160   PROCdrawblock
170 UNTIL X>=1270
180 GOTO 100
190 DEFPROCdrawblock
200  MOVE X,0
210  MOVE X+width,0
220  PLOT 85,X,Y
230  PLOT 85,X+width,Y
240 ENDPROC
```

Fig. 4.15.

The program of *Fig. 4.16* is impressive on a model B machine as it shows all the colours at once.

```
5 REM ALL 16 COLOURS
100 MODE 2
110 colour=0
120 FOR X=0 TO 1279 STEP 320
130   FOR Y=0 TO 1023 STEP 256
140     GCOL 0,colour
150     PROCdrawblock
160     colour=colour+1
170   NEXT Y
180  NEXT X
190 END
200 DEFPROCdrawblock
210  MOVE X,Y
220  MOVE X+300,Y
230  PLOT 85,X,Y+240
240  PLOT 85,X+300,Y+240
250 ENDPROC
```

Fig. 4.16.

42

It is often useful to add text and numbers to graphics or pictures drawn on the screen. It is possible to use the TAB(X,Y) command and print the text where it is required. But the X,Y variables used in TAB are not the X and Y used in graphics. The BBC micro allows either form by two commands which coupled with VDU 5 or un-coupled VDU 4 control the graphics and text cursors.

Two points need to be made here, first that when the cursors are coupled then the graphics colour, specified by the GCOL command, overrides the COLOUR command. The second point is that the VDU 5 command effectively stops the flashing text cursor on the top left of the graphics screen, so tidies up graphic pictures.

So far we have drawn lines and shapes all over the screen. We have moved dots around the screen and we have played with some colours. The next stage is when we start flying. No safety nets now and as a result the commands become ugly, illogical and slightly magic. These are the VDU commands. We have used two so far, VDU 5 and its reverse VDU 4. *Fig. 4.17* lists the others. These control the video processor directly and as a consequence the syntax of each code is specific to that code. Rather than a detailed look at each command, the VDU codes associated with graphics will be looked at in some detail. It is left to the reader to try the other codes using the BBC book as a guide.

VDU 12 will cause the text area to be set to the current back-ground colour and the cursor to go to the top left-hand corner. This is identical to CLS. VDU 16 will clear graphics to current back-ground and is equivalent to the CLG command in BASIC. VDU 17 is identical to COLOUR so VDU 17,2 and COLOUR 2 both set text foreground COLOUR to yellow. Similarly VDU 18 is identical to GCOL. So GCOL 1,3 and VDU 18,1,3 perform the same func-tion.

Now we enter the field of VDU commands that do not have any counterpart in BASIC. VDU 19 allows us to define which colour is associated with a logical colour. Normally we have assumed zero is black, 1 red, 2 yellow and 3 white, but if we have a model A machine or we wish to use a four, or even two, colour mode and want different colours, then we might want zero to be black, 1 to be green and 2 to be flashing red-cyan and 3 to be magneta. The VDU 19 command allows this. The form is:

VDU 19, Logical Colour, Actual Colour, 0,0,0

The three zeros are for future expansion. So VDU 19,1,4,0,0,0 will change Logical Colour 1 from red to 4 which is blue. It will remain so until we change it back or execute a MODE command.

CODE	MEANING
0	Does nothing
1	Send next char to printer only
2	Enable printer
3	Disable printer
4	Separate text/graphics cursors
5	Join text/graphics cursors
6	Enable VDU drivers
7	Make a short beep
8	Backspace cursor one character
9	Forwardspace cursor one character
10	Move cursor down one line
11	Move cursor up one line
12	Clear text area
13	Move cursor to start of line
14	Page mode on
15	Page mode off
16	Clear graphics area
17	Define text colour
18	Define graphics colour
19	Define logical colour
20	Restore default logical colours
21	Disable VDU drivers
22	Select screen mode
23	Re-program display character
24	Define graphics window
25	Plot m,x,y
26	Restore default windows
27	Does nothing
28	Define text window
29	Define graphics origin
30	Home text cursor to top left
31	Move text cursor to x,y
127	DELETE

Fig. 4.17. VDU commands

Let us go to our random triangles program and add more colour. Look at program *Fig. 4.18* and run it. That should convince you of the power of the system. If you get lost or want to get back to nice, safe, understandable colours, then the command VDU 20 will set all colours back to their default condition.

VDU 22 is identical to a **MODE** command, so VDU 22,6 and MODE 6 have the same result. Changing mode sets up default colours so VDU 19 should occur *after* VDU 22.

```
 5 REM RANDOM SHAPES
10 MODE 5
20 X=1280:Y=1024
30 VDU 19,RND(15),RND(255),0,0,0
40 GCOL RND(15),RND(255)
50 MOVE RND(X),RND(Y)
60 MOVE RND(X),RND(Y)
70 PLOT RND(8)+82,RND(X),RND(Y)
80 GOTO 30
```

Fig. 4.18.

The BBC micro allows graphics and text 'windows' to be defined anywhere over the screen. On power up or after a BREAK then both windows are the entire screen. VDU 26 does the same and is the 'panic' VDU command when lost.

Within a graphics window all graphics are visible: outside plot commands remain legal but will not appear. Text is restricted to the text window; scrolling taking place if an attempt is made to write outside the window. To make this obvious let us change the graphics window using the VDU 24 command. The syntax of this is:

VDU 24, left X; lower Y; right X; top Y;

Note the use of semi-colons. These send the decimal number as a byte pair ordered low, high to the processor. So:

VDU 24,50;50;300;300;

would define a window starting at 50,50 and extending to 300,300 and anything 'plotted' would be viewed through this window. VDU 28 lets us do the same sort of thing with the text area of the screen. The VDU 28 syntax is as follows:

VDU 28, left X, lower Y, right X, upper Y

Note that commas are used, unlike VDU 24 commands, and the origin is upper left corner not lower right. The mode will define how large X and Y can be.

To emphasise this very powerful VDU command we will use the program of *Fig. 4.19*. Here we set graphics background to red and text background to yellow. It is well worth while going over this program and understanding it as it is of great use in general graphics programs. The range of graphics commands is exceptional, and exploiting them fully will tax the ingenuity of the most creative designers.

```
100 REM SPLIT TEXT AND GRAPHICS
110 MODE 5
120 VDU 17,130:REM TEXT BGD=YELLOW
130 VDU 17,0  :REM TEXT FGD=BLACK
140 VDU 18,0,129:REM GRAF BGD=RED
150 VDU 18,0,3  :REM GRAF FGD=WHITE
160 VDU 24,0;0;1279;830;
170 VDU 28,0,5,19,0
180 VDU 12:REM CLEAR TEXT SCREEN
190 VDU 16:REM CLEAR GRAF SCREEN
200 FOR K= 1 TO 45
210 PRINT K
220 FOR J=1 TO 1000:NEXT J
230 NEXT K
240 MOVE 0,0
250 DRAW 1279,1024
```
Fig. 4.19.

5
Words

Handling string variables on the BBC micro

In BASIC there are two main classifications of variable—*Numeric* variables and *String* variables. Numeric variables are those numbers referenced by name within a program. String variables are formed from strings of characters such as letters of the alphabet, special symbols such as *, (,),... or the character representation of the integers 0...9. There are two types of numeric variable, integer and real. In this chapter the way in which string variables can be used will be introduced.

What are string variables?

String variables are the way in which items consisting of a series (string) of characters can be represented in BASIC. Each string variable is given a name in the same way that numeric variables are given names, the only difference being that the string variable name must terminate with the $ sign. For example:

   A$, Title$, Christian__name$ and Surname$

are four string variable names, whereas

   A, Title, Age

are three numeric variable names. Notice that A and A$ define two quite separate variables. A is a numeric variable, while A$ is a string variable. Run the program in *Fig. 5.1*, which illustrates how the two are quite distinct.

```
100 REM string and numeric variables
110 INPUT "enter your name " A$
120 INPUT "enter your age " A
130 PRINT:PRINT
140 PRINT "your name is ";A$;" and you are age ";A
150 END
```

Fig. 5.1.

Each string variable may contain up to 255 characters and values may be assigned to string variables in the same three ways as to a numeric variable—that is:

via an INPUT statement;
using the LET statement; or
with the combination of READ and DATA statements.

Using the INPUT statement has been illustrated in the previous program. When assigning data to string variables using either the LET statement or READ-DATA combination, the string to be assigned must be enclosed in a pair of double quotes. For example, see *Fig. 5.2*.

```
100 REMassigning data to string var's
110 LET Title$="Days in January"
120 READ Month$,No_of_days
130 PRINT Title$
140 PRINT
150 PRINT Month$,No_of_days
160 END
170 DATA "January",31

Days in January

January        31
```
Fig. 5.2.

Sometimes we might want quotes " to appear in the text that is assigned to a string variable, in which case for each pair of quotes to appear, two pairs should be entered with the LET or DATA assignment. In the example in *Fig. 5.3* when the variable Quote$ is printed it appears as "Not today thank you"

```
100 REM including quotes in strings
110 READ Quote$
120 PRINT Quote$
130 END
140 DATA """Not today thankyou"""


"Not today thankyou"
```
Fig. 5.3.

Quick summary so far
There are two classifications of variable:

Variables

String	Numeric
e.g. Title$="Demonstration"	e.g. Interest Rate=9.75
Name ends in $	Two types Real and Integer

Each string variable may be up to 255 characters in length.

Operations of string variables

In the same way that numeric variables may be added together, subtracted, tested for equality, etc., so we can perform some of these operations on string variables.

Concatenation of string variable

The equivalent string operation of numeric addition (+) is concatenation—adding one string to another. Run the program in *Fig. 5.4*, in which the variables First$ and Last$ are concatenated for the purpose of neater output.

```
100 REM Concatenation of strings
110 INPUT "Enter your last name "Last$
120 INPUT "Enter your first name "First$
130 Space$="    "
140 Full_name$=First$+Space$+Last$
150 PRINT Full_name$
160 END
```
Fig. 5.4.

To see what would have happened without this concatenation, change line 140 to

140   PRINT First$, Last$

and run the program again. To achieve the same effect as in our original program without concatenation, we would have to have

140   PRINT First$; " "; Last$

The other operators for use with string variables are=, <, >, <=, >=, and <>, their logical meaning being the same as when used with numeric variables. Table 5.1 indicates the use of these operators with string variables, most of which are illustrated in later examples.

Table 5.1. Operators for use with string variables

Operator	Use
+	Concatenation
=	Assignment of one string variable to the current value of another or test of equality
> >= < <=	Sorting string data into alphabetical order
<>	Test of non-equality between the current values of two strings

48

What do we mean by a string of characters?

All the examples so far have used the characters A–Z and a–z, the upper and lower case alphabetic characters. A string variable might also include the numeric characters 0–9. The combined character set A–Z, a–z and 0–9 are often referred to as the alphanumeric character set. In this case the symbols 0–9 are simply characters with the same status as the alphabetic characters and have no numeric value. That is '5' is a character as is '9', 'c', '=' etc. The program in *Fig. 5.5* shows what is meant by this.

```
100 REM numeric characters in strings
110 Number1=12
120 Number2=45
130 Firstnumber$="12"
140 Secondnumber$="45"
150 PRINT "Number1+Number2=";Number1+Number2
160 PRINT "Firstnumber$+Secondnumber$=";Firstnumber$+Secondnumber$
170 END


Number1+Number2=57
Firstnumber$+Secondnumber$=1245
```

Fig. 5.5.

The first of the PRINT statements (line 150) performs a straightforward addition of two numeric variables resulting in the output of 57, the combined total.

The second PRINT statement (line 160) prints out the concatenated string 12 45 where the numeric characters that form the component string values are treated as if they were alphabetic characters—thus having no numeric significance.

Summary

String variables can be operated on in a similar way to numeric variables, the + operator being used to concatenate the values of two or more string variables. Strings may include the numeric characters 0–9, which have no numeric significance or value within the string.

String Functions

In the same way that there are implicit functions in BASIC such as SQR, ABS, INT, etc. to perform operations on numeric variables, so there are functions that make it easy to change the manipulation and alteration of string variables. These string functions fall into the following categories.

1. Functions that relate numeric and string versions of the same data.
2. Functions that provide information about, or determine the contents of, a string variable.
3. Functions that reference parts of a string variable.

There is another group of functions that may be useful when dealing with string or numeric information. These are the functions that relate to the positioning of information on the screen and are described separately in Chapter 4.

Functions that relate numeric and string data

STR$(X)—convert the number X to its string form
Sometimes it is useful to be able to convert numeric data into its equivalent string representation, especially when values are required in a neatly printed form—for example, columns of figures where the decimal point will always be in the same column position. The STR$ function enables us to do this, as shown in *Fig. 5.6.*

```
100 REM the STR$ function
110 INPUT "enter a number "Number
120 PRINT "the number is ",Number
130 PRINT "STR$(Number)=",STR$(Number)
140 END
```
Fig. 5.6.

Notice that when this program is run and the value 9.89 entered, the numeric value when printed is right justified, whereas the string version is left justified. (Right justified means that what is printed is lined up with the right-hand side of the print field.) Apart from this difference you might yet by unconvinced that there is any difference between the output resulting from line 110 and that from line 120. However, if the program is altered so that it includes:

```
120 PRINT "the number is ",Number+3
130 PRINT "STR$(Number)+3=",STR$(Number)+3
```

When the program is run again inputting 9.89, line 120 will result in the output of 12.89– (the value of the original number input +3), whereas line 130 will result in an error 'Type mismatch+line 130'. This error message indicates that we have confused numeric and string values—i.e. we have tried to add the numeric 3 to the string '9.89'.

To correct this error, line 130 must read

```
130 PRINT "STR$(Number+3)=",STR$(Number+3)
```

—that is add ('concatenate') a character 3 to the string version of the original number—the result of this operation is seen in the printing of 9.89—that is 9.89 with '3' concatenated.

The TYPE MISMATCH error is a fairly common one. It always indicates that you have tried to assign a numeric value to a string variable or a string value to a numeric variable.

VAL(A$)—Convert A$ to Numeric form

This function provides the reverse facility to STR$. That is it takes a character string representing a number (A$) and converts it into numeric form. The string must start with a $+$ or $-$ sign, or a number, otherwise VAL will return the value 0. As it returns a numeric value, any printing is right justified. Note *Fig. 5.7.*

```
100 REM The VAL function
110 READ A$,B$,C$
120 PRINT A$+B$+C$
13u PRINT VAL(A$)+VAL(B$)+VAL(C$)
140 PRINT VAL(A$+B$+C$)
150 END
160 DATA "+3.5","-2.5","6.0"
```
Fig. 5.7.

Line 120 results in the concatenated string $+3.5-2.56.0$ being printed, whereas line 130 adds together the numeric values which are then printed as 7 ($=3.5-2.5+6.0$). VAL(A$+B$+C$) attempts to convert the string printed at line 120 to a numeric value but does not print a valid number.

EVAL(A$)—interpret the mathematical expression A$

Although EVAL is a string function its main use is when handling the input of mathematical expressions to a program as it is able to call the part of BASIC that handles mathematical expressions. The simple program in *Fig. 5.8* illustrates this.

```
100 REM the function EVAL
110 A=6;B=4
120 PRINT "A=6 and B=4"
130 PRINT "enter an expression of A and B that has result 2"
140 INPUT Expr$
150 IF EVAL(Expr$)<>2 THEN PRINT "Wrong" ELSE PRINT "Correct"
160 END
```
Fig. 5.8.

The program will not terminate until a correct expression is input (e.g. $A-B$).

The print field width—@%

The print field width setting determines the number of columns covered by the appearance of a ',' in a PRINT statement. The default setting is 10 columns, but this is easily changed by typing @%=n where n is the required field width in columns. n may be any value from 0 to 255—values larger than 255 affect other features such as the number of decimal places to be printed. Details of setting these other parts of @% are given in Chapter 6. The output from both CHR$ and VAL are affected by the current field width setting along with any other values output from a PRINT statement.

Press BREAK (which sets the field width to 10) and run the program in *Fig. 5.9.*

```
100REM the field width control @%
110PRINT 123,123456789,"Numeric"
120PRINT "123","123456789","String"
130END

           123 123456789Numeric
   123        123456789 String
```

Fig. 5.9.

The numeric data (line 110) is printed right justified in 10 column fields, whereas the string data (line 120) is left justified in 10 column fields.

Change the field width to 4 by typing:

>@%=4

and run the program again. The change to a field width of 4 is shown in the new way in which both lines are printed. The field width setting can be changed from within a program with a statement such as:

170 @%=7

This can be extremely useful when tables of information are to be printed, either on the screen or to a printer. Different field width settings can be used within the same program for producing separate output formats for different tables.

Summary

The functions STR$ and VAL are used for translating between numeric and string representations of the same data. When printed, the appearance of string and numeric data are affected by the current field width setting which may be altered by changing the value of the system variable @%, either from within a program or as an immediate statement.

52

Functions that provide information about the contents of string variables

Sometimes information is required about a string variable before we can start to use the string data contained in it. For example, when inserting the value of a string into formatted output we might require the length of the string. Similarly, before sorting string data into alphabetical order we might need to check that all values are in upper case (i.e. check the ASCII code value of individual characters of the string—see the note on the ASCII code in Chapter 8). Functions exist that help in performing such operations.

LEN(A\$)—The length of the string A\$
This function returns the length of the string referred to in its argument (A\$). For example try the following:

```
100 REM the LENgth function
110 INPUT "enter your name " Name$
120 PRINT "your name is ";LEN(Name$);" characters long"
130 END
```

Fig. 5.10.

The length of a string variable includes any spaces embedded within the string—spaces, after all, are just another acceptable character.

ASC(A\$)—Returns the ASCII code value of the first character of the string A\$
The information on the ASCII code in Chapter 8 indicates how each character in the code can be referenced by a decimal value in the range 0–128. For example, referring to the table of ASCII codes in Appendix C, the character 'C' has the decimal code 67, whereas the character 't' has the code 116. These values can be obtained using the ASC function:

```
100 S1$ = "C": S2$ = "t"
110 PRINT   ASC(S1$),  ASC(S2$)
```

Fig. 5.11.

When the argument string of the ASC function is of greater length than one character, the function returns the ASCII character value of the first character of the string. To illustrate this change line 100 to read:

100   S1\$="character": S1\$="test"

and run the program again. Identical values will be returned. Obtaining the ASCII values of the remaining characters in a string will be explained in the section covering the string functions that reference parts (substrings) of a string variable.

The ASC function is useful for converting string data between its upper and lower case forms, as will be necessary when sorting string data alphabetically. It is also useful if we require to selectively mask data input from the keyboard for valid responses. The simple program in *Fig. 5.12* will not be complete until the user enters a '1', a '2' or a '3'.

```
100 REM masking input
110 INPUT "enter 1,2 or 3 "Number$
120 A=ASC(Number$)
130 IF A<49 OR A>51 THEN 110 ELSE END
```

Fig. 5.12.

The ASCII code values for 1, 2 and 3 are 49, 50 and 51 respectively. Notice that the program can be cheated by supplying a number beginning with a 1, 2 or 3. (A way round this can be found with the INKEY function.)

CHR\$(X)—Form a single element string of one character whose ASCII code is X

The reverse function of ASC is provided by CHR\$. This function forms a single element string containing the ASCII character specified by the numeric argument. For example, we found out from the last function that the decimal ASCII code values for 'C' and 't' are 67 and 116. Using the CHR\$ function the reverse operation can be performed:

100   PRINT CHR\$(67), CHR\$(116)

The CHR\$ function is very useful for 'printing' some of the non-printing characters of the ASCII character set. For example, decimal code 7 will sound a beep on the computer's loudspeaker:

>PRINT CHR\$(7)

Other useful codes are:

    10—generates a line feed
    12—clears the screen and homes the cursor to top left
    30—homes the cursor without clearing the screen.

The effect of other non-printing codes can be investigated by referring to the complete ASCII character set in Appendix C.

54

Functions that reference parts (substrings) of string variables

There are three functions that can be used for obtaining substrings from string data.

RIGHT$—refers to the right-hand end of a string.
LEFT$—refers to the left-hand end of a string.
MID$—obtains substrings from the middle of a string.

RIGHT$ (A$,n)
As many characters as required (n) may be obtained from the right-hand end of the string A$. If there are insufficient characters in the string A$ to return n characters, then the entire string will be returned.

LEFT$ (A$,m)
This function is the same as RIGHT$ but for the left-most m characters of the string. The example in *Fig. 5.13* illustrates RIGHT$ and LEFT$ in action.

```
100 REM LEFT$ and RIGHT$
110 READ A$
120 PRINT RIGHT$(A$,8)
130 PRINT LEFT$(A$,3)
140 PRINT RIGHT$(LEFT$(A$,3),2)
150 PRINT LEFT$(RIGHT$(A$,8),4)
160 END
170 DATA "BBC Microcomputer"


Computer
BBC
BC
comp
```

Fig. 5.13.

Try matching the four lines of output to the expressions in lines 120–150.

A further example is the use of LEFT$ to determine the first character of a string in Yes/No response from the user:

```
100 INPUT "Do you want to finish" Response$
110 If LEFT$ (Response$,1) = "N" or LEFT$ (Response$,1) = "n"
    THEN 100 ELSE END
```

Fig. 5.14.

MID$(A$,m,n)—References the middle parts of a string
This useful function can be used for obtaining substrings of characters that are embedded within a string.
For example, the statement

   X$=MID$ (A$,M,N)

will return N characters of the string A$ starting from the Mth character position. If the final parameter N is omitted from the expression, or if there are insufficient characters in the string, then all the string from character position M onwards is returned. Examine the output from the following program to confirm the nature of MID$.

```
100 REM MID$ function
110 A$="BBC Microcomputer"
120 PRINT MID$(A$,5,5)
130 PRINT MID$(A$,3,1)
140 PRINT MID$(A$,10,20)
150 END
```

```
Micro
C
computer
```

Fig. 5.15.

A common use of MID$
Because MID$ can extract any subset of a particular string we can use it for locating individual characters within a string. We might require to know how many words are in a sentence, or how often a particular letter appears—each of these tasks can be accomplished with the aid of MID$. Try the next program that counts the number of words in a sentence input by the user by counting the spaces between words.

```
100 REM counting words in a sentence
110 INPUT "enter a sentence "Sent$
120 Words=1
130 FOR Character=1 TO LEN(Sent$)
140    IF MID$(Sent$,Character,1)=" " THEN Words=Words+1
150    NEXT Character
160 PRINT "Number of words is ";Words
170 END
```

Fig. 5.16.

This program in *Fig. 5.16* is not robust in the sense that extra spaces adjacent to any word in the sentence will increase the word count. Try rewriting the above program so that the present limitations are overcome.

A neater solution to this problem involves using a procedure for handling each word until a trailing space is detected.

INSTR(A$,B$)—Finding the position of a substring B$ within the string A$
The INSTR function allows us to determine where in a string a specific substring occurs. For example, the statement

P=INSTR (A$,B$)

returns a number that corresponds to the character position at which the substring B$ occurs within the string A$. If the substring B$ does not occur anywhere within A$, the INSTR returns a value of 0.

An option exists whereby the character starting position for the search can be specified. The statement

P=INSTR (A$,B$,N)

returns the value of the position of B$ within A$ but with the proviso that the search is started at position N.

Try running the program in *Fig. 5.17.*

```
100 REM the INSTRing function
110 A$="there are the thieves !"
120 B$="th"
130 P=INSTR(A$,B$)
140 PRINT "position of ";B$;" is at character ";P
150 END
```

Fig. 5.17.

Run the program again, first with line 130 as:

130   P=INSTR (A$,B$,5)

and secondly with:

130   P=INSTR (A$,B$,12)

INSTR is powerful function and not usually available in BASIC. It can be used to replace some of the common uses of MID$—MID$ within a FOR . . . NEXT loop can be used to search for individual character or substring positions.

One problem that INSTR can help us with is lining up columns of figures so that the decimal point for each number appears in the same column. After running the program in *Fig. 5.18* you will see that the default numeric output is unsatisfactory.

```
100 REM lining up columns
110 READ Sales,Costs
120 PRINT "Sales",Sales
130 PRINT "Costs",Costs
140 PRINT "Profits",Sales-Costs
150 END
160 DATA 135.56,90
```

```
Sales       135.56
Costs           90
Profits      45.56
```

Fig. 5.18.

Consider what must be done to make the output appear neater with the numbers laid out in correct columnar fashion. Converting the numeric values to their string equivalents using STR$ is the first step, then, for each number, the position of the decimal point should be lined up—numbers with no decimal point will also require consideration. (An alternative approach to solving the same problem involves the setting of @%).

INPUT LINE—A BASIC command very useful for inputting string data
The usual way of getting data into numeric or string variables is with the INPUT statement. However, the problems arise with the INPUT statement if a string is to include commas, quotes or leading spaces. The INPUT LINE statement will accept an entire line of alphanumeric characters, leading spaces, commas, quotes etc until RETURN is entered. Every character preceding RETURN will be included as a valid character within the designated string.

Try the program in *Fig. 5.19*. In response to the prompt to enter a line of data include in your input any or all of leading spaces, commas and quotes.

```
100 REM the INPUT LINE statement
110 PRINT "enter 1 line of words"
120 INPUT LINE A$
130 PRINT:PRINT
140 PRINT A$
150 END
```

Fig. 5.19.

Now run the program again, but with line 120 changed to

120   INPUT A$

Error messages will possibly be generated when the same input is attempted. Leading spaces will be ignored and so will every item after the first comma.

With this comprehensive set of functions for handling strings the layout of text and of tables of values is made much easier.

6

Numbers

Simple mathematical functions

Run the program in *Fig. 6.1*, which introduces the functions ABS, SGN and INT.

```
100  REM ABSolute,SIGN and INTeger functions
110 FOR I=1 TO 2
120    READ Number
130    PRINT "ABS(";Number;")=";ABS(Number)
140    PRINT "SGN(";Number;")=";SGN(Number)
150    PRINT "INT(";Number;")=";INT(Number)
160    NEXT I
170 END
180 DATA -33.45,57.99
```

```
ABS(-33.45)=33.45
SGN(-33.45)=-1
INT(-33.45)=-34
ABS(57.99)=57.99
SGN(57.99)=1
INT(57.99)=57
```

Fig. 6.1.

These functions operate in the following ways:

ABS (X)—returns the absolute value of the argument X. In the above example ABS(-33.45) is 33.45 but ABS(57.99) is 57.99 since a positive value is its own absolute value. One use of ABS is to find the magnitude of the difference between two numbers when it is not known which is the larger. Try typing PRINT ABS(A$-$B) to illustrate this.

SGN (X)—indicates the sign of the argument X according to

-1 if X is negative
  0 if X is zero
$+1$ if X is positive

In our example SGN(-33.45) returns -1 whereas

SGN (57.99) returns +1. One way of finding the larger of the two numbers would be to use SGN to return the sign of the difference between the two numbers. In the example program an additional PRINT SGN (A–B) will reveal whether the difference is positive, negative or zero.

INT (X) —produces the integer part of the number X, −34 in the case of INT(A) and 57 for INT(B). No rounding occurs (INT(57.99)=57), and the argument X is simply truncated to the nearest integer smaller than X itself.

A common use of INT is when numbers need to be manipulated to a limited number of decimal places. The example program in *Fig. 6.2* rounds off the number N to two decimal places, printing the result, R:

```
100   N=231.57984
110   R=INT(N*100+.5)/100
120   PRINT R
130   END
```

Fig. 6.2.

The next two functions are concerned with the result of dividing one whole number by another:

MOD—gives the remainder after division.
DIV —gives the whole number part of the result of a division.

For example the following results would be obtained from using DIV and MOD

15 DIV 3=5 and 15 MOD 3=0
14 DIV 3=4 and 14 MOD 3=2

These functions are useful if we require a program that will convert numbers to different base arithmetic values, or when breaking down a number into its component parts. For example, the program in *Fig. 6.3* reveals the value of the low byte of the 32 bit integer N%:

```
100 REM the MOD function
110 N%=255
120 L%=N% MOD 256
130 PRINT L%
140 END
```

Fig. 6.3.

The SQR(X) function

BASIC includes a function for obtaining the square root of a number. Its use can easily be illustrated in the command mode: enter PRINT SQR(4) at the terminal and the result 2 will be displayed.

Generating random numbers

Most versions of BASIC have a function that generates a series of random numbers, useful in games programs and some areas of statistics.

RND generates a random whole number in the range −2147483648 to 2147483647.

RND(X) generates a random whole number in the range 1–X (including X), whilst RND(1) generates a random number between 0 and .999999. The program in *Fig. 6.4* will generate a series of five random numbers between 1 and 10:

```
100 REM generating random numbers
110 FOR I=1 TO 5
120    PRINT RND(10)
130    NEXT I
140 END
```

Fig. 6.4.

To generate truly random numbers the random number generator should be randomly set before any numbers are produced. For example, inserting the line:

90   X=RND (−RND(100))

will ensure that the random number generator is randomly set before each run of the program.

RND (−X)—returns the value −X and resets the random number generator to a value based on X.

The next set of functions enables the values of the logarithmic mathematical functions, logs base 10, natural logs and exponentials, to be obtained The functions are:

LOG(X) returns the log base 10 (common logarithm) of the value X.

LN(X)   returns the log base e (natural logarithm) of X.

EXP(X)   calculates the value of e^x. That is 2.7183 raised to the power X.

The program in *Fig. 6.5* shows how LOG(X) and LN(X) might be used to produce a table of values for a range of X:

61

```
100@%=&00020407
110 REM the logarithmic functions
120 PRINT "X","LOG(X)","LN(X)"
130 FOR X=1 TO 10
140   PRINT X,LOG(X),LN(X)
150   NEXT X
160 END
```

```
X       LOG(X) LN(X)
 1.0000 0.0000 0.0000
 2.0000 0.3010 0.6931
 3.0000 0.4771 1.0986
 4.0000 0.6021 1.3863
 5.0000 0.6990 1.6094
 6.0000 0.7782 1.7918
 7.0000 0.8451 1.9459
 8.0000 0.9031 2.0794
 9.0000 0.9542 2.1972
10.0000 1.0000 2.3026
```

Fig. 6.5.

A later program in the book shows how graphs of mathematical functions can be drawn.

Trigonometric functions

The BBC BASIC has a wide range of functions associated with obtaining the value of the trigonometric functions sine, cosine and tangent. They are:

PI   returns the value of Pi (3.14159265) e.g. Pi *R^2 calculates the area of a circle, radius R.

DEG(X)   converts angles, (X), that are expressed in radians into degrees.

RAD(X)   converts angles, (X), expressed in degrees into their radian measure equivalent.

SIN(X)
COS(X)   the trigonometric functions which return the sine, cosine
TAN(X)   or tangent value of X, where X is expressed in radians.

ASN(X)
ACS(X)   the inverse trigonometric functions which return the angular value (in radians) that correspond to a function
ATN(X)   value of X.

                 The range of X for ASN and ACS is $-1 \leqslant X \leqslant 1$ and for ATN $-1E38 \leqslant X \leqslant 1E38$.

Although the value returned by ASN etc. is in radians it is easily converted to degrees with the DEG function. Similarly, when using the trigonometric functions SIN, COS and TAN a radian value for X is easily supplied by converting from a degree value with the RAD function.

The example program in *Fig. 6.6* prints a table of the sine, cosine and tangent function values in the range 0–180° in 30° steps. @% has been used to control the print format.

```
100 REM the trigonometric functions
110 @%=&00020307
120 PRINT "Angle","Sine","Cosine","Tangent"
130 FOR Ang=RAD(0) TO RAD(180) STEP RAD(30)
140   PRINT DEG(Ang),SIN(Ang),COS(Ang),TAN(Ang)
150   NEXT Ang
160 END
```

```
Angle  Sine  Cosine Tangent
  0.000 0.000  1.000   0.000
 30.000 0.500  0.866   0.577
 60.000 0.866  0.500   1.732
 90.000 1.000  0.0002.14748365E9
120.000 0.866 -0.500  -1.732
150.000 0.500 -0.866  -0.577
180.000 0.000 -1.000  -0.000
```

Fig. 6.6.

PRINT field formatting—@%

It is easy to change the PRINT column field width setting by changing the value of @%. Any value between 0 and 255 may be used as a column width setting.

e.g. @%=40

forces a field width setting of 40 columns. (This means that on a 40 column display each item in a print statement will appear on a new line if a comma appears between items in the PRINT statement.)

Other features of @%
@% is an integer variable and therefore occupies a total of four locations in memory. Only one of these locations, that corresponding to

the least significant part of @%, is concerned with the field width. The contents of the other three locations each have their own specific purpose. An example of setting @% which makes use of all of its features is shown in *Fig. 6.7.*

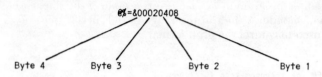

Fig. 6.7.

Byte 1 is as already described the PRINT field width setting (i.e. number of columns);
Byte 2 determines the number of digits printed in the various formats as selected by byte 3;
Byte 3 selects one of the three basic formats, General (G), Exponent (E), or Fixed (F);
Byte 4. If byte 4=1, strings created using STR$ are printed as though they are numeric values according to the current setting of @% (but left justified), otherwise, values are printed as conventional string values.

Formats available using byte 3 are selected by 0, 1 or 2. The effect of the setting of byte 2 depends on the format setting as follows:

Byte 3	*Byte 2*
0–General Format	Maximum number of digits to be printed before Exponent format is used.
1–Exponent Format	Number of digits +1 that is to follow the E
2–Fixed Format	Number of decimal places

The programs in *Figs 6.8* and *6.9* illustrate the three possible formats and the effect of each on particular values for bytes 1, 2 and 4.

Logical functions

Functions exist in BBC BASIC for performing the standard logical operations of AND, OR, NOT and EXCLUSIVE OR (EOR) between two values. These functions may be used in two quite distinct ways—either as logical operators or as a bit by bit operator.

```
100 REM controlling the print format
110 A=104.294:B=17.482:C=0.039
120 @%=&00000209:REM General format
130 PRINT A,B,C
140 @%=&00010209:REM Exponent format
150 PRINT A,B,C
160 @%=&00020209:REM Fixed format
170 PRINT A,B,C
```

```
      1E2        17    3.9E-2
   1.0E2     1.7E1    3.9E-2
    104.29    17.43     0.04
```

```
100  REM the effect of byte 4 on STR$ values
110  REM fixed format, 2 dec places, fieldwidth=9
120  @%=&01020209
130  PRINT 17.678
140  PRINT STR$(17.678)
150  @%=&00020209
160  PRINT STR$(17.678)
170  END
```

```
    17.68
17.68
17.678
```

Fig. 6.8.

```
100  REM the effect of byte 4 on STR$ values
110  REM exponent format, 2 dec places, fieldwidth=9
120  @%=&01010209
130  PRINT 17.678
140  PRINT STR$(17.678)
150  @%=&00010209
160  PRINT STR$(17.678)
170  END
```

```
    1.8E1
1.8E1
17.678
```

Fig. 6.9.

Logical operators

These are used most commonly in an IF construct, although other
uses are possible. For example if a program were to perform some
action if the variable AGE=35 and SEX$=Male, and to perform
some other action if this was not the case, the following statement
might appear in the program:

65

```
IF AGE=35 AND SEX$="MALE" THEN  . . . . . . . . . . . . . . . . .
            . . . . . . .   ELSE . . . . . . . . . . . . . . . . . . . .
```

Similarly we might have:

```
IF AGE=35 OR AGE=36 AND SEX$="MALE" THEN  . . . . .
            . . . . . . .   ELSE . . . . . . . . .
```

To select 35 or 36 year old males.

Bitwise operations

The logical functions can also be used to perform bitwise operations between values. An example of a bitwise logical AND between the binary values of 0110 (decimal 6) and 0101 (decimal 5) is:

```
      0110      (6 dec)
      0101      (5 dec)
AND  0100      (4 dec)
```

That is a 1 AND 1 produces a 1 in the result and any other pair combination of 0 and 1 produces a 0 (0 AND 0,0 AND 1, 1 AND 0).

As BBC BASIC integers are 32 bits long, the effect of a bitwise AND between the variables X and Y, where X=7 say and Y=4, is:

```
      X 00000000 00000000 00000000 00000111   (7 dec)
      Y 00000000 00000000 00000000 00000100   (4 dec)
X AND Y 00000000 00000000 00000000 00000100   (4 dec)
```

In describing the AND operation above we have really only defined its truth table:

A	B	A AND B
0	0	0
0	1	0
1	0	0
1	1	1

The bitwise logical operations of the OR, EOR (Exclusive OR) and NOT functions act in a similar way according to the definition of the OR, EOR and NOT operations. That is according to the truth tables:

A	B	A AND B	A OR B	A EOR B
0	0	0	0	0
0	1	0	1	1
1	0	0	1	1
1	1	1	1	0

A	NOT A
0	1
1	0

Thus for the decimal numbers 6 and 5, bitwise logical operations on 4 bits produce:

```
        0110                    0110
        0101                    0101
6 OR 5  0111  (7)      6 EOR 5  0011  (3)
```

NOT 6 is NOT(0110)=1001 (9); NOT 5 is NOT(0101)=1010 (10).

The NOT operation will turn all 0s to 1s and vice versa. This means that in the case of an integer variable of 32 bits all 0s to the left of the most significant 1 will be complemented (i.e. become 1s). Thus in 32 bits NOT (5 dec) is:

```
NOT 00000000 00000000 00000000 00000101
  = 11111111 11111111 11111111 11111010
```

The logical functions AND, OR etc., perform in exactly the same way whether used as logical operators or in a bitwise fashion. That is their effect on data variable values is always a bitwise one. However, in logical operations such as might appear within an IF construct expressions are first evaluated to either TRUE or FALSE where:

```
     TRUE = 11111111 11111111 11111111 11111111
and  FALSE= 00000000 00000000 00000000 00000000
```

For example, if A=3
    IF A=3 OR A=5 THEN ....   ELSE ....

evaluates to TRUE

A bitwise OR between TRUE (111 . . . etc.) and false (000 . . . etc.) then results in 111 . . . (TRUE) which means that the THEN part of the construct will be executed.

TRUE and FALSE are the names of functions in BBC BASIC with the above binary values. In decimal, the statement:

    PRINT   TRUE,   FALSE

will result in −1 and 0 respectively being printed.

There is no easy division of what are string functions and what are numeric functions in that programs that deal with numeric data are quite likely to use string functions as well as the more obvious numeric functions. Much of the conventional use of string functions to control the printing of output is not required if the powerful features of @% are utilised.

7
Sound

The SOUND command can be used to give four independent channels of output. Three of the channels are tone channels, the fourth is a noise generator. The command requires four parameters which give control over channel number, frequency, loudness and duration of the tone produced, i.e. the format is:

100 SOUND control, loudness, freq, duration

where:

control is a multifunction parameter which can be considered as a four digit hexadecimal number, where each digit performs a different function. The least significant digit is used to select the channel, and the other three are used for some additional functions which will be described in more detail later. This channel select digit can take any value from 0 to 3, and since the other digits have no effect when they take the value 0, *control* can be considered, simply, as an integer from 0 to 3 when it is used to select the channel.

control is 0 to select the noise generator, and 1, 2 or 3 to select the tone channels.

loudness controls the sound intensity and can have a value from 0 to −15 for zero to maximum respectively. This parameter can also take a positive value from 1 to 4, when the envelope (loudness, attack, decay) is determined by the definition of up to four ENVELOPE statements. There is also an adjustment for maximum volume on the circuit board of the computer.

freq determines the pitch of the sound produced and can take any value from 0 to 255, covering just over five octaves. The value 4 produces the note C one octave below middle C, and steps of 4 give steps of one semitone in pitch.

duration determines the length of time the sound effect is sustained and again can take any value from 0 to 255. The highest figure will produce a continuous sound which can be turned off by using one of the extended features of *control*. The duration of the sound produced is 50 ms times the value of this parameter.

An example is given in *Fig. 7.1*, which plays the first three notes of a well known tune, when the program is RUN:

```
50 SOUND1,-15,68,10
60 SOUND1,-15,60,10
70 SOUND1,-15,52,20
```

Fig. 7.1.

Since the four channels are independent, it is possible to play chords, using the SOUND command. An example of this is given in *Fig. 7.2*.

```
100 SOUND 1,-15,52,40
110 SOUND 2,-15,68,40
120 SOUND 3,-15,80,40
```

Fig. 7.2.

Elements of music

The musical scale is divided into octaves where the frequency ratio of the top note to the bottom note is $2:1$. The interval of each octave is divided into 12 equal parts called semitones. Scales are produced by moving up this semitone scale in various different steps of semitones and double semitones, or tones. For example, the major scale is produced by the following steps from the base note to that one octave above:

Tone, Tone, Semitone, Tone, Tone, Tone, Semitone

If all the notes from one C to the next are listed and given numbers as indicated:

C C# D D# E F F# G G# A A# B C — note names
1 2 3 4 5 6 7 8 9 10 11 12 13 — note numbers.

Then the scale of C major would consist of the notes 1,3,5,6,8,10,12,13. The semitones between the notes of the scale above are shown as sharps, but they could equally have been shown as flat notes. This numerical cross reference for notes can be used within a program as will be shown later on, when the notes of a tune are translated into a list of numbers which permit the tune to be played.

Since the third parameter of SOUND, i.e. freq, will produce semitone steps for steps of 4 in its value, the program in *Fig. 7.3* will play a major scale. The first data item, 52, will determine the key of the scale, which in this case is C major.

```
100 REPEAT

110 READ freq

120 SOUND 1, -15, freq, 40

130 UNTIL freq = 100

140 END

150 DATA 52,60,68,72,80,88,96,100
```

Fig. 7.3.

The insertion of a PRINT statement between lines 120 and 130 viz. 125 PRINT freq will show the effect of the buffering of frequency values as the first six values are printed immediately the program is started, then the buffer is full and the remaining notes are read only when one note has been completed. Another feature of this note buffer is that the tune is still playing when the cursor re-appears to indicate that the computer is ready.

The above ideas can be used to write a simple program (listed in *Fig. 7.4*) which will play a melody for which notes and time values are read from DATA statements at the end of the program. It is however more convenient to set up a number system for the notes as indicated earlier, and to make it possible to enter time values which are related to the time value of the actual notes.

An array of 25 elements is set up which covers two octaves including all semitones. The bottom note is specified in line 120 as the value 52 (middle C), which is stored in scale(1). The other notes are built up from this base note. Since this value is chosen to produce a C, the notes and array element numbers will correspond with the note names and numbers given earlier, with the addition of numbers from 14 to 25 for the second octave.

The unit of beat is specified so that the DATA statement can contain numbers corresponding to the time values of the notes to be played, and if the tempo is wrong only this variable needs to be changed.

Provision is made for rests in the tune to be played and a short rest note is used between notes to separate them, and to allow for two separate notes at the same pitch.

The data for the tune is read from DATA statements at the end of the program, the information being read directly from the music as indicated. The last two data items are dummy items which are used to terminate the program.

71

```
100 DIM scale(25)
110 FOR I = 1 TO 25
120   scale(I) = 52+4*(I-1)
130   NEXT I
140 beat = 8
150 REPEAT:loop=1
160   READ note,length
170   IF note = 99 THEN END
180   t = beat*length
190   IF note=0 THEN SOUND1,0,0,t ELSE SOUND 1,-15,scale(note),t
200   SOUND1,0,0,1
210   UNTIL loop=0
220 END
230 DATA 3,1/2,8,3,10,3,12,5,0,1/2,12,1/2
240 DATA 13,2,13,1,12,3/2,8,1/2,12,1,10,5,0,1/2,3,1/2
250 DATA 5,3,7,3,8,2,10,1/2,12,1/2,5,1,10,3/2,13,1/2
260 DATA 12,3,10,3,8,5,0,1/2
270 DATA 99,0 :REM data terminator
```

Fig. 7.4.

The program shown will play the tune *Plaisir D'Amour* with the
DATA statements shown (key G major: 3/4 time). The first few bars
of this tune are shown in *Fig. 7.5.*

Fig. 7.5.

The SOUND command is more complex than has been described
previously. The first parameter (control) can be used to specify more
than the channel number. To consider these additional functions it
is more convenient to consider this parameter as a four digit hexadecimal number as mentioned above.

		r	s	b	c
i.e.	&	#	#	#	#

c— the least significant digit is that used to select the channel
number, as described above.

b— is the note buffer control and can be 0 or 1; 0 is the default condition.

1 removes any notes in the buffer and stops the note currently
being played

s— is the simultaneous note control and can take the values 0, 1, 2
or 3. In the chord example, when the chord is played a slight
delay occurs between the start of the first note and the start of
each subsequent note. This digit can be used to prevent this

72

delay between notes which should be played simultaneously and, instead, hold up 0, 1, 2 or 3 notes so that 1, 2, 3 or 4 notes can be started simultaneously.

r— is used to produce no sound (a rest). It takes the value 0 for normal SOUND command operation. The value 1 produces no output from that channel but allows any decaying sound to be heard from a preceding note.

To illustrate some of these features consider first the clear buffer facility. If a note is produced with a duration of value 255, the note will continue until the escape button is pressed.
e.g. type:

SOUND 1,−15,100,255   then hit the RETURN key

This should now play a continuous tone.
Now type in

SOUND 1,−15,60,40   and press RETURN.

There should be no change. If, however, the same command is entered with the clear buffer option active, the continuous tone should stop and the new note will play.
i.e.

SOUND &11,−15,60,40

The simultaneous note control is best demonstrated by a program which plays a broken chord, by inserting time delays between the different notes of the chord. This program is shown in *Fig. 7.6*. RUN it and hear what happens.

```
100 SOUND 1,-15,52,40
110 PRINT1
120 PROCdelay
130 SOUND 2,-15,68,40
140 PRINT2
150 PROCdelay
160 SOUND 3,-15,80,40
170 PRINT3
180 END
190 DEF PROCdelay
200 FOR I=1 TO 1000: NEXT I
210 ENDPROC
```

Fig. 7.6.

The delay is long enough to make the chord sound more like three overlapping notes!

Modify the control parameter of SOUND in each command, by putting &020 in front of the channel number. The delays exist as before and the three numbers are printed after each SOUND command is read, but the chord is now played as a chord immediately after the last note is read. (See *Fig. 7.7.*)

```
100 SOUND &0201,-15,52,40
110 PRINT 1
120 PROCdelay
130 SOUND &0202,-15,68,40
140 PRINT 2
150 PROCdelay
160 SOUND &0203,-15,80,40
170 PRINT 3
180 END
190 DEF PROCdelay
200 FOR i=1 TO 1000:NEXT i
210 ENDPROC
```

Fig. 7.7.

Envelope control

The SOUND command, as it has been described above, will produce only a constant amplitude note. It is also possible to have sounds with attack, sustain and decay sections determined by another BASIC statement, ENVELOPE. Up to four different amplitude shapes can be set up using this statement and the second parameter of SOUND, normally used for loudness, can be used to select one of the four envelopes using a positive number from 1 to 4 to make the selection.

ENVELOPE is used as a BASIC command with 14 parameters. It does not do anything on its own but is called into play by the SOUND command. A typical ENVELOPE statement would be:

100   ENVELOPE en, stp, ptstpl, ptstp2, ptstp3, nstps1, nstps2, nstps3, rate1, rate2, rate3, relr, bp1, bp2

where the 14 items separated by commas are the parameters of this particular BASIC function. Unused parameters are given the value zero. The parameters are defined below.

en (envelope number) is an integer of value 1, 2, 3 or 4 which determines the envelope used by SOUND when its second parameter, loudness, is 1, 2, 3 or 4 respectively.

stp (step size) is used to set the step size for all the time-dependent features of ENVELOPE. It is an integer from 1 to 127 which gives a step size of 10* stp in milliseconds.

ptstp 1, 2 and 3 (pitch step 1, 2 and 3) are used with
nstps 1, 2 and 3 (number of steps 1, 2 and 3) respectively, to pro-

74

vide up to three frequency ramps in the output of the SOUND command.

ptstp sets the change in pitch. This can be a positive or negative number from -128 to $+127$, where each step of four is a semitone as for the frequency parameter of SOUND. The starting value of the pitch will be determined by the SOUND command.

nstps sets the number of pitch changes, the duration of each being determined by the parameter *stp*. *nstps* can have a value from 0 to 255.

rate1, *rate2* and *rate3* determine the rate of change of amplitude over three sections from the start to *bp1*; from *bp1* to *bp2*; and from *bp2* until the end of the sound, determined by the *duration* of SOUND. The unit of time for the three rates is the step size defined by *stp*.

rate1 is positive and can take a value from 1 to 127.

rate2 can be positive, zero, or negative from -127 to $+127$.

rate3 can be any number from -127 to 0.

bp1 and *bp2* are the breakpoint levels at the end of the first and second sections respectively and can each vary from 0 to 126.

relr (release rate) determines the rate of decay of the sound after the time specified by *duration* in SOUND. This will only be heard if no new note is started after this note is completed, or if the next note is a dummy note.

The amplitude parameters are summarised in *Fig. 7.8*.

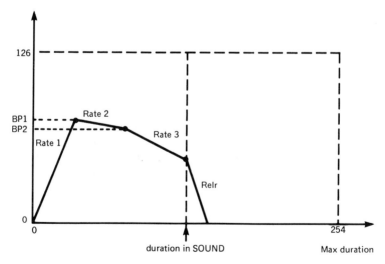

Fig. 7.8.

The ENVELOPE command is illustrated in the simple program in *Fig. 7.9* which uses the pitch step facilities to play up and down part of a scale with a single SOUND command. The first pitch step is zero and produces the base note of the SOUND command.

```
90ENVELOPE 1,50,0,8,-8,1,2,3,126,0,0,-126,126,126
100SOUND 1,1,60,50
```

Fig. 7.9.

The noise generator

Channel 0 of the SOUND command is used to produce noise rather than tones as for the other three channels. The numbers used to control the operation of the channel also operate in a slightly different way from those of the tone channels. The first parameter is used as described before to select the channel, loudness and duration are also used in the same way. The parameter used to select frequency, however, does not operate with values from 0 to 255 as before but uses the numbers from 0 to 7 instead. 0, 1 and 2 produce motor boat type noise at three different frequencies, 0 giving the highest frequency. *Fig. 7.10* illustrates the use of this particular way of using SOUND:

```
100 FOR I=0 TO 2
110 SOUND 0,-15,I,40
120 NEXT I
130 END
```

Fig. 7.10.

This will produce the three different frequencies one after the other.

When the number 3 is used for the frequency parameter the SOUND command in channel 0 does not produce any sound output on its own. It requires, instead, an additional SOUND command in channel 1 which determines the frequency of the noise generator output. The channel 1 statement need not produce any output of its own but must have a duration which is the same as that of the channel 0 statement. The program in *Fig. 7.11* will produce three notes on the noise generator, where the pitch is determined by the SOUND commands in line 120:

```
100 FOR I=0 TO 2
110 SOUND 0,-15,3,40
120 SOUND 1,0,100+8*I,40
130 NEXT I
140 END
```

Fig. 7.11.

76

The effect with the number 100 in line 120 is very like the note of an engine. If, however, this number is changed to 200 the sound produced is more musical in quality.

The effects just described for channel 0 when its frequency parameter is varied from 0 to 3 are repeated for the values 4 to 7, except that white noise is produced. The values 4, 5 and 6 produce three different frequencies as before, the lowest frequency being produced by the value 4. When the value 7 is used the noise generator requires the additional SOUND command, on channel 1, to determine the frequency of the sound output on channel 0.

The program in *Fig. 7.11* with line 110 altered to be:

110   SOUND 0,−15,7,40

will illustrate the kind of noise produced by using this value for the frequency parameter.

The BASIC variable ADVAL can be used to obtain information on the buffer space for the SOUND channels. ADVAL (−k) where k is 5, 6, 7 or 8 gives respectively the number of free spaces in the buffers for Channel 0, 1, 2 or 3, e.g.

PRINT ADVAL (−6)

will give a value of 15 when the buffer is empty.

8
Bits and bytes

The programs so far have concentrated on BASIC and rightly so in view of the very satisfying version provided. Occasional use has been made of routines and information involving specific memory addresses. Many of the special functions in the graphics and I/O areas implicitly use such routines to achieve speed and efficiency.

In Chapters 8 and 9 we look at how such routines can be written and where and why they are used. To do this needs some understanding of the way instructions and data are stored as codes: there are many good books on this subject and we restrict ourselves to selecting enough to give a flavour of the topic. The principles are common to all microprocessors but the examples given are specific to the 6502. The microprocessor used, the 6502, is at the heart of the Apple, Pet, Atari, VIC and most of the low-cost machines for the educational and consumer markets.

Memories and bus systems

All information is stored in the memory of microcomputers as a pattern of 0s and 1s. Storage cells called flip-flops, organised into groups of eight, have output voltages that switch between 0 V and 5 V to represent these values. Each cell represents a logical quantity called a BIT, and the group of eight cells represents a BYTE.

BIT No. 7 6 5 4 3 2 1 0
         0 1 1 0 1 1 0 0
         Logical quantity: Byte=8 Bits

Each group of eight cells has a unique code number giving its location or address, carried by an address bus of 16 lines which again take the values of 0 or 1 (0 V or 5 V) at different instants. The address bus is connected to all the memory which may be organised on different integrated circuits. At any one instant only one memory location will be active, responding to its own 16 bit code. Similarly, each memory cell is linked to the appropriate line of the 8 bit data bus. For example, bit 3 of 10,000 different memory locations will be connected to line 3 of the data bus, but only one of them will respond and accept the data on that line. It is *not* necessary to have the 2^{16} or 65,536 physical memory locations present—this is merely the maximum number that can be handled.

The address bus is said to be unidirectional in that the address is fed to the memory circuit from outside (normally from the central processing unit or CPU of the microprocessor). Data can be written into as well as read from much of the memory, i.e. the data bus is bidirectional. This kind of memory, instead of having the logical name READ-WRITE MEMORY, is still called RAM or random access memory. This property of random access it shares with the other main type of memory, ROM, or read only memory, used to permanently store standard programs or data.

Each byte of memory stores an 8 bit binary number, giving $256=2^8$ possibilities. This number has no meaning in itself, but we can write programs in which the number in the first address is the code for some action to be taken on the number stored in the second, third or subsequent addresses. We can therefore have up to 256 distinctly different actions performed by the micro and it can cope with data in the range 0 to 255.

Hex numbers and machine code

It is very awkward to deal with 8 bit or 16 bit binary numbers. A more convenient method of representing them is in hex code. Hex stands for hexadecimal, i.e. numbers counted in 16s rather than 10s in the decimal system to which we are used, and 2s in the binary system of the micro itself. Hex is a compromise: it is an unfamiliar but compact way of representing binary numbers by grouping them four bits at a time. A group of four bits has $2^4=16$ possible values varying from 0000 to 1111. We let the numbers 0 to 9 stand for the first ten of these possibilities and the letters A to F for the remaining six. This is an arbitrary but now accepted choice.

Binary	Hex	Dec
0000	0	0
0001	1	1
0010	2	2
.	1	1
.	1	1
1001	9	9
1010	A	10

Binary	Hex	Dec
1011	B	11
.	.	.
.	.	.
1111	F	15

Numbers larger than 15 then require two digits in the same way as do numbers above 9 in the decimal system. Thus

Hex		Dec
10	$(1\times16)+(0\times1)$	16
18	$(1\times16)+(8\times1)$	24
1F	$(1\times16)+(15\times1)$	31
FF	$(5\times16)+(15\times1)$	255

Thus two-digit hexadecimal numbers from 00 to FF cover the eight-digit binary numbers from 00000000 to 11111111 and the decimal values from 0 to 255.

The BBC micro will accept both decimal and hex numbers. Since it is not always clear whether a number is decimal or hexadecimal, the computer must be told which type of number it has been given. This is done by prefixing all hex numbers with the & symbol.

Here are a few examples using hex numbers:

(i) LET N=&41
assigns the value hex 41, i.e. decimal 65, to N, equivalent to LET N=65.

(ii) FOR N=0 TO & 1F
The counter N would range from 0 to hex 1F or decimal 31.

Converting hex to decimal/decimal to hex

Some people can perform these conversions in their head, others use tables, but there is no need for either technique. What are computers for if not to make life easy? Your micro will happily carry out this task.

To print the decimal value of a hexadecimal number such as &FFFF, type

PRINT &FFFF

The computer will reply with its decimal value, namely 65,535 and unless told otherwise will give all its answers in decimal. Try the following:

(i) PRINT &1F+&AA
(ii) PRINT 25+&AA
(iii) PRINT 4 * &FF

To perform a conversion in the opposite direction, decimal to hexadecimal, the ~ symbol or tilde is used. This symbol has the meaning 'IN HEXADECIMAL'.

PRINT ~ 16

will give the result 10.

(It is worth noting that in Mode 7, the teletext mode, the symbol appears as a ÷ symbol on the screen.)

Try the following example:

PRINT ~ & 102A

Since the statement means PRINT IN HEXADECIMAL THE HEXADECIMAL NUMBER 102A, the computer displays 102A.

Numbers for characters—The ASCII code

Your computer works with numeric information, namely the numbers between 0 and 255. How then does it recognise non-numeric characters in variable names or strings? The answer is simple: it uses a coding system where each letter of the alphabet and special character, such as +, /, $, #, etc., is given a numeric value. The most common system used by microcomputer manufacturers is known as the American Standard Code for Information Interchange, or ASCII code. A table of this coding system is given in Appendix C. However, your computer can help you translate back and forth between ASCII codes and characters.

Characters to ASCII code
The function ASC finds the ASCII code corresponding to a character, e.g. to find the ASCII code for A type:

PRINT ASC("A")

The computer will give the answer 65 which is the code for A in decimal. If you wish the code in hex, then type:

PRINT ~ ASC("A")

You should obtain the answer 41. Try a few other characters yourself. Check your answers with those given in Appendix C.

ASCII code to characters
To translate from ASCII to character, the CHR$ statement is used.

PRINT CHR$(65)

will give the result A.

It is also possible to convert hexadecimal codes to characters.

PRINT CHR$(&41) should also give A.

The BBC micro has a useful feature where PRINT and CHR$ functions can be combined into a single statement called VDU. The following instruction will give the same result as the example above.

VDU 65

Examination of the ASCII table in Appendix C shows that not all the 256 possible codes are required to represent the common symbols found on most typewriters. The extra codes, called control codes, have been given special jobs in the BBC micro. For example, VDU 30 moves the cursor to top left corner of the screen, VDU 7 makes a short bleep. We will look at some of these codes in more detail in the following chapter.

Displaying 'hidden messages'

Your computer contains many messages stored as lists of ASCII characters ocupying consecutive memory locations in the read only memory (ROM) chips. For example, at switch-on the message 'BBC Computer 16K (32K)' appears on the screen. This message is stored in memory from location &DB13 upwards. (This might change in later versions of the machine.) The short program in *Fig. 8.1* uses the CHR$ statement to display the message while giving the address, and its contents in hex, of each character in the message. *Fig. 8.2* shows the output.

```
10 REM TO DISPLAY  BBC Computer 16K"
20 REM *****************************
30 FOR N=&DB13 TO &DB23
40 PRINT ~N,~?N,"   ",CHR$(?N)
50 NEXT N
```

Fig. 8.1.

There are many more messages in the system ROMs. The program in *Fig. 8.2* should help you find them. It scans through the entire 32K of ROM looking for messages. Two points are worth noting.

(a) Only characters with ASCII codes between &20 and &7F are displayed. This prevents 'strange effects' occurring on the screen due to some of the BBCs special codes.

82

DB13	42	B
DB14	42	B
DB15	43	C
DB16	20	
DB17	43	C
DB18	6F	o
DB19	6D	m
DB1A	70	p
DB1B	75	u
DB1C	74	t
DB1D	65	e
DB1E	72	r
DB1F	20	
DB20	0	
DB21	31	1
DB22	36	6
DB23	4B	K

Fig. 8.2.

(b) Obviously not all of the characters displayed on the screen are part of a meaningful message. Most of the characters displayed are part of the operating system machine code program.

```
5REM TO DISPLAY "HIDDEN MESSAGES"
6REM*****************************
10 FOR N=&8000 TO &FFFF
20 A=?N
30 IF A>&20 AND A<&7E THEN PRINT CHR$(A);
40 NEXT N
```

Fig. 8.3.

```
LL @BASIC(C)1981Acorn%ARW3X#LANDABSACSADVALASCASNATNAUTOBGETBPUTCOLOURCALLCHAINCH
R$CLEARCLOSECLGCLSCOSCOUNTDATADEGDEFDELETEDIVDIMDRAWENDPROCENDENVELOPEELSEEVALER
LERROREOFEQRERREXPEXTFORFALSEFNGOTOGET$GETGOSUBGCOLHIMEMCINPUTIFINKEY$INKEYINTIN
STR(LISTLINELOADLOMEMCLOCALLEFT$(LENLETLOGLNMID$(MODEMODMOVENEXTNEWNOTOLDONOFFOR
OPENINOPENOUTPRINTPAGECPTRCPIPLOTPOINT(PROCPOSRETURNREPEATREPORTREADREMRUNRADRES
TORERIGHT$(RNDRENUMBERSTEPSAVESGNSINSQRSPCSTR$STRING$(SOUNDSTOPTANTHENTOTAB(TRAC
ETIMECTRUEUNTILUSRVOUVALVPOSWIDTHPAGEPTRTIMELOMEMHIMEMP+2Vx&OdxUUh_- =7999 $aal3
&W^P/bWZ439)YFC9K89x!csAC1r4r%$SAAAAJJLLLPPRSSS>OL2II%)*OONNN>XHh(@~8xOPp!AaF&f
```

Fig. 8.4. Output from program in Fig. 8.3

Inserting characters

You will already have used a method for inserting characters into memory locations—namely assigning values to string variables.

e.g.   10   A$="FRED"

When the computer meets this statement it will store away a list of ASCII characters for the letters FRED in consecutive memory locations at the end of your program, i.e. above TOP. However, there is a method that allows messages or strings of characters to be placed

83

anywhere in the system memory. Obviously, care must be taken not to place the message in the middle of a program.
E.g. the statement

$ &1500="ABC"

would place the ASCII codes for ABC into memory locations &1500, &1501, &1502. The character string defined by the inverted commas can be up to 128 characters long.

Try the example program in *Fig. 8.5* which inserts a message from &1500 upwards then displays it.

```
10REM ****PLACING MESSAGES****
20REM*
30REM*
40 MESSAGE=&1500
50 $MESSAGE="J.D.FERGUSON"
60 FOR N=0 TO 11
70 PRINT CHR$( ?(&1500 +N));
80 NEXT N
90 END


RUN


J.D.FERGUSON
```

Fig. 8.5.

Examining/changing memory locations

Unlike most other dialects of Basic, the BBC micro does not have PEEK or POKE statements. It uses instead the ? or query operator to perform the same functions, allowing you to examine or change the contents of a memory location. It stands for 'THE CONTENTS OF' and should be followed by the address of the location. Thus:

PRINT ? &FFFF

will look at the contents of memory location &FFFF and print its value in decimal. If we wished an answer in hex, the statement would be:

PRINT ~ ? &FFFF

meaning 'PRINT IN HEXADECIMAL THE CONTENTS OF HEXADECIMAL ADDRESS FFFF'. It is often convenient to look at the contents of a block of memory locations. The program in *Fig.*

84

8.6 will print the address and the contents of 20 memory locations starting at &F000.

```
10 FOR N = 1 TO 20
20 X = &F000 + N
30 PRINT ∿ X,∿? X
40 NEXT N
```

Fig. 8.6.

The value of N is added to the base address &F000 to give the address of the memory location which is then printed together with its contents in hex.

The query operator can also be used to alter memory locations. However, a word of caution is due. Changing memory locations used by the machine operating system may result in a loss of control of the machine from the keyboard, requiring the BREAK key to regain control. A safe location to alter is &1500. First use the query operator to print its contents. The value there will probably be whatever was in the memory when the computer was switched on. To change the contents of this location to 6, type:

? &1500=6

i.e. 'THE CONTENTS OF HEXADECIMAL ADDRESS 1500 EQUALS 6'.
To verify that the change has occurred, type:

PRINT ? &1500

A second operator '!' or pling allows you to change or examine memory locations 'four at a time'. Since each memory location contains an 8 bit byte, this operator handles 4×8 or 32 bit numbers. Like the query operator, it should be followed by an address, which this time acts as a starting address for 4 memory locations. Thus:

PRINT ∼ ! &F000

which reads 'PRINT IN HEXADECIMAL THE CONTENTS OF 4 MEMORY LOCATIONS STARTING AT HEX ADDRESS F000' would give the 32 bit hexadecimal number 60C904F4.

The order in which the 4 bytes are displayed is:

The contents of F000—60
The contents of F001—C9
The contents of F002—04
The contents of F003—F4

85

In a similar manner to the query operator the pling can be used to alter memory locations. Thus:

!&1500=& AA018844

would place:

AA into 1500
01 into 1501
88 into 1502
44 into 1503

Try the example in *Fig. 8.7*.

```
10REM****PLING ! *******
20REM*
30REM  USE TO INSERT 4 BYTES
40 !&1500=&12345678
50REM  USE TO EXAMINE 4 BYTES
60 PRINT ~!&1500
70REM  NOTE HOW LAST BYTE GOES INTO
80REM  FIRST MEMORY LOCATION
90 PRINT ~?&1500
100 PRINT ~?&1501
110 PRINT ~?&1502
120 PRINT ~?&1503
130 END


RUN


12345678
      78
      56
      34
      12
```

Fig. 8.7.

9
Assembly language

The 6502 microprocessor

The 6502 is the 'brains' of the computer containing all the logic required to recognise and execute the list of instructions called the program. All the time the machine is switched on the microprocessor is busy, reading numbers from memory, interpreting them as instructions and then carrying out the operations specified by these instructions. To help it with this task there are a number of special memory locations, called registers, on the microprocessor chip itself. These are identified by name rather than number, i.e. they are not part of the so-called Memory Map.

The registers of the 6502 are indicated in *Fig. 9.1*.

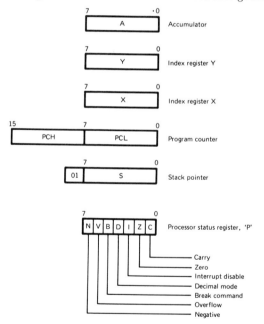

Fig. 9.1.

The accumulator A is the register involved in most of the mathematical and logical functions because of its greater power than other registers and memory locations. The X and Y registers are used to store values for counting, timing and indexing (identify an address or sequence of addresses referenced to some base address and particularly useful in scanning tables of values with the minimum of programming). The program counter, PC, registers the current address; the stack pointer keeps records of information put aside when the microprocessor is temporarily diverted from its main task, and the status register is a collection of individual bits identifying features of the previous instruction.

The program followed by the microprocessor bears little resemblance to BASIC. The only language the processor understands is the language of 0s and 1s, or MACHINE CODE. For example, the set of binary numbers below forms a short machine code program that stores the number 21 (hex) in memory location 1600 (hex):

Binary	In Hex Representation
10101001	A9
00100001	21
10001101	8D
00000000	00
00010110	16

Some of these numbers are called OPERATION CODES or 'OP CODES', and tell the processor what it has to do. In the example, A9 tells the processor to load its accumulator with the next number, namely 21. The next code, 8D, tells it to store the contents of the accumulator in location 1600 (hex), the memory location defined by the next two numbers.

Although it is possible to write programs directly in machine code (in some early microcomputers it was the only method, e.g. KIM), it is a slow process, prone to error, requiring the programmer to make continuous reference to instruction tables similar to those shown in Appendix D. An alternative approach is to write programs in a more 'human friendly' format called ASSEMBLY LANGUAGE. This language uses alphabetic abbreviations for each type of instruction rather than binary or hex OP codes. For example, abbreviations such as LDA and STA are used to represent the operations LoaD the Accumulator and STore the Accumulator. These abbreviations are often called 'mnemonics' because they are more easily remembered than OP codes. Written in mnemonics, the example program becomes:

LDA #21
STA 1600

The question now arises, 'How does this assembly language program become the machine code program stored in the computer's memory?' The answer is to use a special program called an ASSEMBLER which translates the 'easily understood by humans' assembly program into the language of the processor, machine code.

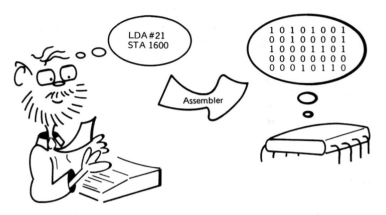

Fig. 9.2. Assembler

Using the assembler

Entering an assembly language program on the BBC micro is similar to entering a BASIC program. There are some extra instructions required that can best be explained with the aid of an example (*Fig. 9.3*).

```
10 P% = &1500
20 [
30 LDA #&21
40 STA &1600
50 RTS
60 ]
```

Fig. 9.3.

—Line 10 acts as an 'origin' statement for the program, telling the assembler where the machine code has to be positioned in the computer's memory. The integer variable P% is used for this task.
—Lines 20 and 60 contain square brackets (they appear as arrows in MODE 7) that enclose the Assembly Language program.

—Line 30 contains the instruction to LoaD the Accumulator with 21 (hex).

—Line 50 contains a ReTurn from Subroutine instruction which returns control to BASIC on completion of the machine code program.

The RUN command will assemble the program, placing the machine code in memory. An assembler listing of the mnemonics and the machine code will also be sent to the display.

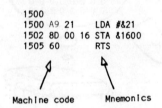

```
1500
1500 A9 21    LDA #&21
1502 8D 00 16 STA &1600
1505 60       RTS
```

Machine code   Mnemonics

Fig. 9.4.

Examination of memory location &1600 will show that the program has not yet been executed. Try:

PRINT ~ ? &1600

i.e. it is unlikely that it contains &21.

To execute the machine code program we use the CALL statement followed by the starting address of the routine, i.e. type:

CALL &1500

The computer will execute the program and return to BASIC, displaying the '>' prompt. Check memory location &1600 again. It should now contain &21.

The CALL statement can be included at the end of the program, see *Fig. 9.5.*

```
10 P% = &1500

20 [

30 LDA #&21

40 STA &1600

50 RTS

60 ]

70 CALL &1500
```
Fig. 9.5.

90

On the command RUN the program will be assembled and then executed.

Comments and labels
Documentation considerably improves a program, making it easier to read. In BASIC, comments are added using REM statements. Unfortunately REM statements are not allowed within the assembler program and comments must be attached to assembler statements using a semi-colon or backslash (\)

e.g.   40   STA &1600; THIS IS A COMMENT

Variable names can be used to represent memory addresses or memory contents. However, they must be defined outside the square brackets holding the assembler program

e.g. NUMBER=&21
     STORE   =&1600

An exception to this rule is the definition of program addresses. If we wished to label the starting address of a program 'START' it could be done as follows.

    30   START LDA #&21

The label is prefixed by a full stop (period) '.' and separated from the assembler mnemonic by at least one space.

Using comments and labels the previous program becomes that listed in *Fig. 9.6.*

```
 10 REM ************************
 20 REM DEMO ASSEMBLER PROGRAMME
 30 REM ************************
 40 P%=&1500
 50 NUMBER=&21
 60 STORE=&1600
 70 [
 80 .START LDA #NUMBER ;GET NUMBER
 90        STA STORE ;STORE NUMBER
100        RTS   ;BACK TO BASIC
110 ]
120  CALL START
```

Fig. 9.6.

Finally a word of caution on the choice of labels. The same restrictions are placed on variable names as in BASIC. In particular, BASIC 'keywords' like PRINT, NEXT, REPEAT, END, etc. are definitely NOT ALLOWED. However, their lower case equivalents are permitted.

91

Operating systems subroutines

The BBC micro's operating system ROM contains many useful machine code subroutines that can be included in your assembler program. Three routines of particular interest are:

1. OSRDCH—OPERATING SYSTEM READ CHARACTER
   Address— &FFEO:
   Reads a character from 'the input channel', normally the keyboard, placing it in the accumulator.
2. OSWRCH—OPERATING SYSTEM WRITE CHARACTER
   Address—&FFEE:
   Writes a character in the accumulator 'down the output channel', normally to the screen.
3. OSASCI—OPERATING SYSTEM ASCII Address—&FFE3:
   As for OSWRCH except that a line feed is automatically inserted with a carriage return.
   (Note: The X and Y registers are not affected by any of these routines.)

The example in *Fig. 9.7* turns the computer into an electronic typewriter that will ignore all BASIC keywords and merely display depressed keys on the screen. The subroutine OSRDCH is used to obtain the ASCII code of any depressed key. OSASCI then transfers this code from the accumulator to the display. The JMP START instruction sends the processor back to the keyboard to look for another depressed key.

```
1 OREM ************************
20REM USING THE OS SUBROUTINES
30REM ************************
35 DIM SPACE 100
40 OSASCI=&FFE3
50 OSRDCH=&FFEO
60 P%=SPACE
70 [
80 .START JSR OSRDCH ;GET CHART. FROM KB
90         JSR OSASCI ;PLACE ON SCREEN
100        JMP START ;REPEAT
110 ]
120  CALL START
```

```
OF22
OF22 20 EO FF .START JSR OSRDCH ;GET CHART. FROM KB
OF25 20 E3 FF JSR OSASCI ;PLACE ON SCREEN
OF28 4C OF JMP START ;REPEAT
```

Fig. 9.7.

In this example we have used a different technique to instruct the assembler where to position the machine code. Rather than defining uniquely where the code has to be placed, the DIM statement in line

35 reserves 101 bytes and places the machine code in this reserved space at the end of the BASIC program. This technique has the advantage that the assembler will ensure that the machine code program is positioned in a safe place within the system memory and will not corrupt either the original BASIC program or memory locations allocated to the screen.

Two pass assembly

The BBC assembler uses the full stop to define labels within an assembly program. However, problems arise when a label is referred to before it is defined. This situation is illustrated in the example in *Fig. 9.8* where the 'typewriter' program has been modified to return control to BASIC whenever the asterisk key is depressed:

```
35 DIM SPACE 100
40 OSASCI=&FFE3
50 OSRDCB=&FFE0
60 P%=SPACE
70 [
80.START JSR OSRDCH  ;GET CHART. FROM KB
85        CMP #ASC"*" ;IS IT AN "*"
87        BEQ FINI    ;IF SO QUIT
90        JSR OSASCI  ;PLACE ON SCREEN
100       JMP START   ;REPEAT
105.FINI RTS          ;RETURN TO BASIC
110 ]
120 CALL START
```

Fig. 9.8.

The label FINI appears in line 87 but is not defined until line 105. An attempt to assemble the program would give the result shown in *Fig. 9.9*

```
0F28
0F28 20 E0 FF .START JSR OSRDCH ;GET CHART. FROM KB
0F2B C9 2A    CMP #ASC"*" ;IS IT AN "*"

No such variable at line 87
```

Fig. 9.9.

—namely the assembler stops, displaying an error message. The solution is to allow the assembler to pass through the source program twice. In the first pass the assembler establishes a table of labels and their addresses. In the second pass it uses these addresses to construct the final machine code program. Due to the assembler being 'embedded' in BASIC, the extra programming required to initiate the two pass assembly is relatively simple, requiring only a FOR . . . NEXT loop to sent the assembler through the program twice, see *Fig. 9.10.*

```
FOR N = 1 TO 2

P% = SPACE

[
```
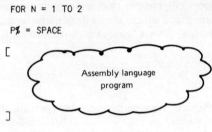
Assembly language program
```
]

NEXT N
```

Fig. 9.10.

However two points are worth noting:

(i) The equate statement for the origin P% must be enclosed within the loop so that it is reset to the correct value at the start of each pass.

(ii) A 'OPT' statement is required to suppress error messages and prevent the assembler halting during the first pass. A number between 0 and 3 is used with this statement to give the following options during assembly:

OPT0 assembler errors suppressed, no listing
OPT1 assembler errors suppressed, listing
OPT2 assembler errors reported, no listing
OPT3 assembler errors reported, listing

A reasonable choice of options might be OPT1 during the first pass to suppress error messages and OPT3 during the second pass to display any errors still remaining. This is achieved in the example in *Fig. 9.11* by placing the counter N after the OPT statement in line 70 and assigning it the values 1 and 3 in line 55:

```
 35 DIM SPACE 100
 40 OSASCI=&FFE3
 50 OSRDCH=&FFE0
 55 FOR N=1 TO 3 STEP 2
 60   P%=SPACE
 70   [OPTN
 80   .START JSR OSRDCH ;GET CHART. FROM KB
 85          CMP #ASC"*" ;IS IT AN "*"
 87          BEQ FINI    ;IF SO QUIT
 90          JSR OSASCI  ;PLACE ON SCREEN
100          JMP START   ;REPEAT
105   .FINI RTS          ;RETURN TO BASIC
110   ]
115      NEXT N
120 CALL START
```

Fig. 9.11.

94

With these options the assembler produces a listing on the display during each pass. However the relative displacement of 06 at &0F4C is only resolved in the second listing.

```
OF46               OPTN
OF46 20 E0 FF  .START JSR OSRDCH  ;GET CHART. FROM KB
OF49 C9 2A      CMP #ASC"*"  ;IS IT AN "*"
OF4B F0 FE      BEQ FINI     ;IF SO QUIT
OF4D 20 E3 FF  JSR OSASCI    ;PLACE ON SCREEN
OF50 4C 46 0F  JMP START     ;REPEAT
OF53 00         .FINI RTS    ;RETURN TO BASIC
OF46               OPTN
OF46 20 E0 FF  .START JSR OSRDCH  ;GET CHART. FROM KB
OF49 C9 2A      CMP #ASC"*"  ;IS IT AN "*"
OF4B F0 06      BEQ FINI     ;IF SO QUIT
OF4D 20 E3 FF  JSR OSASCI    ;PLACE ON SCREEN
OF50 4C 46 0F  JMP START     ;REPEAT
OF53 60         .FINI RTS    ;RETURN TO BASIC
```

Fig. 9.12.

A final point worth noting is the use of the statements VDU 14 and VDU 15 to switch the 'PAGE MODE' on and off. This can prove useful when assembling large programs to examine the assembly listing a page or 'screenful' at a time.

Mixing machine code and BASIC

Two statements allow control to pass to a machine code routine from BASIC—'CALL' and 'USR'. With both statements the processors A, X, and Y registers are initialised to the least significant bytes of the integer variables A%, X% and Y% and the carry flag is set to the least significant bit of the variable C% on entry to the machine code routine.

e.g.   10   A% = &41   10   A% = &41
        20   CALL &FFEE   20   Z = USR(&FFEE)
        30   END   30   END

Each of these programs would send 41 hex or ASCII 'A' to the display routine OSWRCH at FFEE hex.

On completion of the machine code routine USR return a 32 bit number made up of the processor's status, Y, X and A registers. For example, see *Fig. 9.13.*

The CALL statement offers greater flexibility, allowing program variables of all types to be passed to and from a machine code subroutine. To aid this transfer a 'parameter block', starting at &0600,

```
  1 OREM ***************************
  2 OREM DEMO OF THE "USR" FUNCTION
  3 OREM ***************************
 40 DIM SPACE 100
 50 P%=SPACE
 60 [
 70 LDA #&AA ;SET A=&AA
 80 LDX #&BB ;SET X=&BB
 90 LDY #&CC ;SET Y=&CC
100 SEC      ;SET CARRY =1
110 RTS      ;RETURN TO BASIC
120 ]
130 RESULT=USR(SPACE)
140 PRINT~RESULT


OF35
OF35 A9 AA    LDA #&AA ;SET A=&AA
OF37 A2 BB    LDX #&BB ;SET X=&BB
OF39 A0 CC    LDY #&CC ;SET Y=&CC
OF3B 38       SEC      ;SET CARRY =1
OF3C 60       RTS      ;RETURN TO BASIC
  BICCBBAA
  ⌣ ⌣ ⌣ ⌣
  /  |  |  \
  P  Y  X  A
```

Fig. 9.13.

contains details of the number, location and type of variables to be passed. The block has the following structure:

    0600—number of parameters
    0601—low byte of address 1st parameter
    0602—high byte of address 1st parameter
    0603—code defining parameter type
    0604—low byte of address 2nd parameter
    0605—high byte of address 2nd parameter
    0606—code defining parameter type
    etc.

The codes used to define parameter types are:

      0—8 bit byte (e.g. ?X)
      4—32 bit integer variable (e.g. X%)
      5—40 bit floating point number (e.g. T)
    128—A string at a defined address (e.g. $X)
    129—A string variable (e.g. A$)

In the example in *Fig. 9.14* the structure of the parameter block is illustrated by passing two variables, B% and C%, in the subroutine CALL to &FFEE in line 60:

96

```
10 B%=&00112233
20 C%=&44556677
30 A%=&55
60 CALL&FFEE,B%,C%
70 FOR N=&0600 TO &0610
80 PRINT~?N
90 NEXT N
```

Fig. 9.14.

Lines 70 to 90 print details of the start of the parameter block in hex:

Address 0600 contains 02 − number of variables

0601	,,	08	ADL 1st variable
0602	,,	04	ADH 1st variable
0603	,,	04 − code for integer variable	
0604	,,	0C	ADL 2nd variable
0605	,,	04	ADH 2nd variable
0606	,,	04 − code for integer variable	
		FF	
		etc.	

Investigating &0408 and &040C, we find the values of the two variables B% and C% (*Fig. 9.15*).

```
100 FOR N=&0408 TO &040F
110 PRINT~?N
120 NEXT N
```

Fig. 9.15.

The final example illustrates a machine code program that will convert and display decimal numbers between 0 and 255 as binary. The program begins by assembling and inserting the machine code program. A small BASIC program then calls the conversion utility, passing the parameter NUMBER % which is then displayed in binary.

```
    10 DIM BINARY 100 ,TEMP 4
    20 OSASCI=&FFE3
    30 FOR N=0 TO 2 STEP 2
    40   P%=BINARY
    50 [OPTN
    60     LDY #00 ;SETY=0
    70     LDA &0601 ;TRANSFET POINTERS TO ZERO PAGE
    80     STA &80
    90     LDA &0602
   100     STA &81
   110     LDA (&80),Y ;GET NUMBER
   120     STA TEMP ;PLACE IN TEMPORARY STORE
   130     LDX #08 ;USE COUNTER TO EXAMINE 8 BITS
   140 .START BIT TEMP ;"1" OR "0"
   150     BPL ZERO ;BRANCH IF ITS A ZERO
   160     LDA #ASC"1" ;PRINT "1"
   170     JSR OSASCI  ;TO DISPLAY
   180     JMP ROTATE
   190 .ZERO LDA #ASC"0" ;PRINT "0"
   200     JSR OSASCI
   210 .ROTATE ROL TEMP ;ROTATE BYTE LEFT
   220     DEX   ;NEXT BIT
   230     BNE START
   240     LDA #0D ;C-RETURN TO DISPLAY
   250     JSR OSASCI
   260 ]   RTS     ;BACK TO BASIC
   270 ]
   280 NEXT N
   290 REM **************
   300 REM BASIC PROGRAMME
   310 REM TO GENERATE
   320 REM BINARY NUMBERS
   330 REM **************
   340 FOR NUMBER%=0 TO 16
   350   CALL BINARY,NUMBER%
   360     NEXT NUMBER%
   370 END
   >RUN
00000000
00000001
00000010
00000011
00000100
00000101
00000110
00000111
00001000
00001001
00001010
00001011
00001100
00001101
00001110
00001111
00010000
```

Fig. 9.16.

98

Driving graphics from machine code

All the BASIC keywords used to control the display have their equivalent VDU statement, e.g:

PRINT "A" is the same as VDU 65
MODE 5   is the same as VDU 22,5
COLOUR 3 is the same as VDU 17,3

etc.

The link between the BASIC VDU statement and operating system display routine OSWRCH is easily understood if the keyword 'VDU' is interpreted as 'SEND THE FOLLOWING BYTE (S) TO OSWRCH', i.e. the assembly language equivalent of

(a) PRINT "A" or VDU 65 is: LDA #65
                                     JSR OSWRCH
(b) MODE 5 or VDU 22,5 is: LDA #22
                                       JSR OSWRCH
                                       LDA #5
                                       JSR OSWRCH

The VDU statements use all 32 ASCII control codes (i.e. ASCII codes not used as symbols or alphanumeric characters). The first byte after the VDU statement, i.e. the first byte sent to OSWRCH, selects the desired display function. The operating system then knows how many more bytes are required to complete the instruction, e.g. MODE selection only requires one byte after the code, whereas redefining the shape of a display character requires 9.

The example program in *Fig. 9.17* selects the display mode.

```
 10 REM ********************
 20 REM SELECTING SCREEN MODE
 30 REM FROM AN ASSEMBLY
 40 REM LANGUAGE ROUTINE
 50 REM ********************
 60 OSWRCH=&FFEE
 70 DIM SPACE 100
 80 INPUT"WHICH MODE"M
 90 P%=SPACE
100 [
110 LDA #22    ;CONTROL CODE FOR MODE SELECT
120   JSR OSWRCH ;DOWN OUTPUT CHANNEL
130   LDA #M     ;SELECT MODE
140   JSR OSWRCH ;DOWN OUTPUT CHANNEL
150   RTS        ;BACK TO BASIC
160 ]
170 CALL SPACE
180 PRINT "THIS IS MODE";M
190 END
```

Fig. 9.17.

Using control codes as a means of selecting and driving different display functions adds greatly to the BBC micro's flexibility. It can be adapted as a colour graphics terminal communicating through either its RS423 serial port to a larger mainframe computer, or through its own system bus, called the 'Tube', to a second processor option.

10

Interfacing—time and space

The interface to physical systems

When any type of computer is used in a monitoring and control application it becomes more closely associated with the system to which it is connected than when it is being used purely to manipulate data.

One effect of this is that program execution time is important since all input data must be obtained on a regular basis and calculated values must be presented either to the human operator or to the system control elements as the events occur, since safe or correct operation of the system can be at risk if this does not happen.

To achieve the link between the computer and the system, it is necessary to present physical data from the system in a machine readable form and to output data to the control elements in such a way that correct control is achieved.

The basic facilities of the BBC microcomputer in this application area will now be described, together with some simple examples illustrating their use.

The analogue interface

Typical physical measurements which have to be made include temperature, pressure and fluid flow. These are all quantities which can take an infinite number of different values over the range imposed by the constraints of the system. For example in measuring water temperature in an unpressurised system, the range of temperatures is 0° to 100°C, and heated water can have a temperature anywhere in this range.

Such quantities are known as analogue quantities and can be measured using sensors and electronic circuits which produce outputs in the form of voltages or currents proportional to the variable being measured.

The computer can, however, only make sense of binary data, i.e. voltage levels which are treated as ones and zeros. Some form of conversion circuitry is therefore required to change continuously variable voltages (or currents) to groups of binary digits which can be dealt with by the processor.

The BBC micro is provided with such conversion circuitry in the form of a four-channel analogue-digital converter integrated circuit. Each channel accepts a voltage input and, under control of the operating system of the computer, converts the analogue data to binary and stores the result in memory. Separate memory locations are used for the information from each channel.

The analogue to digital converter takes about 5 ms to perform a conversion from one channel. The operating system scans each channel automatically at 10 ms intervals and updates the values stored in memory.

The converter produces a 12-bit digital output, so more than one memory location has to be used for each channel. Two locations are used and the 12 bit data is placed at the most significant end of this space with the four remaining bits held at zero.

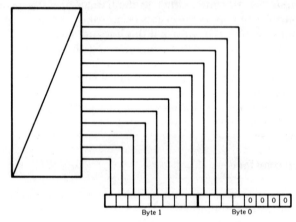

Fig. 10.1. Analogue/digital converter

The range of the analogue/digital converter output is thus 0–4095 and since it is placed, as described, in a 16 bit format the range of the stored data is:

    0–4095*16
  i.e. 0–65520

The BASIC variable which permits the analogue data to be read and then manipulated in a program is:

  ADVAL (n)

102

where the parameter n can take the value 1, 2, 3 or 4, corresponding to the four channels.

For example

    100   PRINT ADVAL (1)

would display on the screen the current stored value of the data from channel 1.

In order to read analogue data it is necessary to connect signals to the input lines brought out to the 15-way D-type connector on the rear of the microcomputer.

The relevant pins on this connector are:

Channel 1   —Pin 15
Channel 2   —Pin 7
Channel 3   —Pin 12
Channel 4   —Pin 4
Reference voltage—Pins 11 and 14
Analogue ground—Pins 5 and 8
Zero volts   —Pins 2, 3, and 6: +5 volts—Pin 1

The information given above is slightly modified from that given in the current users' guide, which uses a numbering system for the channels which does not correspond with the numbers used in the ADVAL command.

The reference voltage required for the analogue-digital converter is generated on board, and is brought to two of the pins of the 15-way connector as indicated. An input voltage which is equal to this reference voltage will produce a full scale reading.

A simple circuit which will permit the four channels to be tested is shown in *Fig. 10.2*, while a program which can be used with this arrangement is shown in *Fig. 10.3*.

The program in *Fig. 10.3* alters the print format variable @% to display only two decimal places of any number. The screen is cleared and four channel messages are printed.

The 'ADVAL' readings are scaled to read from 0 to 100%, and are placed alongside the messages. A delay, determined by the FOR . . . NEXT loop, occurs before the analogue channels are read and displayed again.

The REPEAT . . . UNTIL loop is continuous, and the program will stop only on pressing the escape key. Since @% is altered and not restored, all numbers printed will appear in two decimal place format (even line numbers). This can be restored to normal by pressing the Break key.

The reference voltage is obtained from a simple circuit of three diodes and a resistor connected in series across the 5 V supply. This

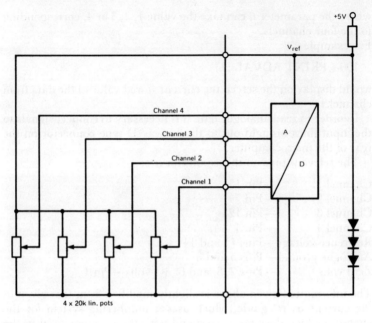

Fig. 10.2.

```
100 @%=&0002020A
110 MODE4
120 PRINT TAB(0,4)"CHANNEL 1 % :-"
130 PRINT TAB(0,8)"CHANNEL 2 % :-"
140 PRINT TAB(0,12)"CHANNEL 3 % :-"
150 PRINT TAB(0,16)"CHANNEL 4 % :-"
160 k=100/65520
170 x=0
180 REPEAT
190 a=k*ADVAL(1)
200 b=k*ADVAL(2)
210 c=k*ADVAL(3)
220 d=k*ADVAL(4)
230 PRINT TAB(17,4) a
240 PRINI TAB(17,8) b
250 PRINT TAB(17,12) c
260 PRINT TAB(17,16) d
270 FOR I=1 TO 500: NEXT I
280 UNTIL x=1
```

Fig. 10.3.

does not give the 2.5 V reference as stated in the users' guide, instead
the voltage is about 1.8 V. Thus the full-scale value of any analogue
channel will be obtained with this voltage. The internal circuit is
shown in *Fig. 10.4.*

104

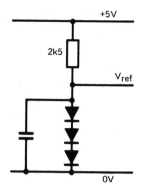

+5V

2k5

V_{ref}

0V

Fig. 10.4.

If an alternative and more satisfactory reference is desired, the diodes could be removed and replaced by one of the stable voltage reference devices, producing 1.25 V or 2.5 V.

The digital interface

The versatile interface adaptor (VIA) of the BBC micro has one of its two ports brought out to a connector on the main circuit board. This port is available to the programmer for input or output of binary information.

The VIA is connected to the processor buses in such a way that it appears at memory addresses FE60–FE6F, the addresses of the user port and its data direction register are FE60 and FE62 respectively.

The ? command can be used to transfer data to and from these registers as part of a BASIC program.

The data direction register data placed at FE62 will set corresponding bits of the port to output where a '1' is entered and to input where a '0' is entered.

The program in *Fig. 10.5* will produce a binary up counter with a frequency determined by the number of counts in the FOR ... NEXT loop:

```
100  ?&FE62=&FF
110  ?&FE60=0
120  x=0
130  count=0
140  REPEAT
150    ?&FE60=count
160    count=(count+1) MOD 256
170    FOR i=1 TO 100 : NEXT i
180    UNTIL x=1
```

Fig. 10.5.

The first instruction places a '1' in each bit position of the data direction register and thus makes each bit of the port an output. The dummy variable, x, is used to ensure that the REPEAT . . . UNTIL loop will run continuously.

The variable count is incremented by 1 modulo 256, to ensure that its value will always be in the range 0–255 or 00000000 to 11111111, in binary. In order to observe this output, connections will have to be made to the port pins and some means of display provided. A suggested circuit is shown in *Fig. 10.6*.

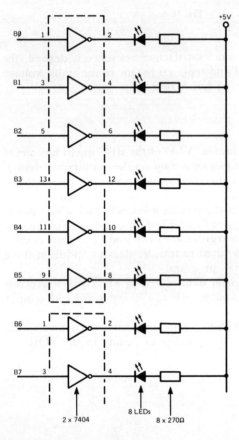

Fig. 10.6. Count display

Timing events

One of the facilities provided in the BBC micro's version of BASIC gives an indication of elapsed time. This internal timer, which is updated every 10 ms, can be read and set using a variable TIME.

To set this variable to any particular value, it is treated as any other variable in the program, e.g.

100   TIME=0

would set the timer to zero, after which time its value would increase by one every 10 ms.

At any later time the value of TIME can be accessed and, for example, printed on the screen:

200   PRINT TIME

Since TIME is updated on an interrupt to the microprocessor, then it will continue to update independently of any program which is running in the micro and can be used to determine the execution time of the program to the nearest 10 ms. For example, see *Fig. 10.7.*

```
100 @%=&00020208
110 MODE 4:REM clears screen
120 TIME=0:REM resets TIME
130 PRINT TIME
140 FOR I=1 TO 5
150    s=SQR(I)
160    PRINT s,TIME
170    NEXT I
180 PRINT "test finished"
190 PRINT TIME
200 END
```

Fig. 10.7.

The program computes the square roots of the numbers from 1 to 5 and the timer value is printed alongside the square root each time. This will give an indication of the speed of execution of the program. One additional timer value is included after the last PRINT command, but any number could be included. An example of the print-out on the display is shown in *Fig. 10.8.*

```
>RUN
    0.00
    1.00    3.00
    1.41    6.00
    1.73    8.00
    2.00   11.00
    2.24   14.00
test finished
   16.00
```
Fig. 10.8.

Figs 10.7 and *10.8* give an example, the principles of which can be applied to any situation. It is more useful to use this facility when writing programs such as those introduced below, in which the time taken to execute a particular routine is of relevance to the correct operation of the program.

The TIME variable can be used to set up a simple program which will execute on a regular basis and, for example, log input data. The kernel of such a system keeps track of time and allocates time-slots for the different computations. To keep the program simple, elapsed time can be displayed in seconds only, even though it is more usual to display time of day in such systems on a 12 or 24 hour clock.

Consider *Fig. 10.9.*

```
100 TIME = 0
110 q = 0
120 sec = 0
130 PROConesec
140 oldq = q
150 REPEAT
160 q = (TIME DIV 25) MOD 4
170 sec = TIME DIV 100
180 UNTIL q = (oldq + 1) MOD 4
190 IF q = 0 THEN PROConesec
                ELSE PROCqsec
200 GOTO 140
210 END
300 DEFPROCqsec
310 ....
320 ....
350 ENDPROC
400 DEFPROConesec
410 PRINT TAB(0,4)"Elapsed Time:-",sec;"secs"
420 ....
430 ....
450 ENDPROC
```

Fig. 10.9.

The PROC sections are not shown completely, for simplicity, but will be expanded later. The procedures are intended to be executed on a regular basis:

PROCqsec every 250 ms
PROConesec every second

The program starts by setting initial values for TIME, q—the quarter second counter, and sec—the one second counter. q counts in modulo 4, so starting at 0 it will count 0, 1, 2, 3, 0, 1– – – – –. The instructions inside the REPEAT . . . UNTIL loop update q and sec, until q has increased by one modulo 4 (using oldq to check that this has occurred). q will increase by one every 25 units of the variable TIME, i.e. every 250 ms.

If the instructions in the program loop were to take less than 10 ms to execute there would be 25 cycles round the REPEAT ... UNTIL loop. As this execution time increases, the number of cycles in the loop will decrease to ensure that line 190 is entered every 250 ms. Since q will be 0 every second, the procedure PROConesec will be executed at the start of each new second. PROCqsec will, instead, be called every 250 ms.

It is essential for the maximum execution time in the program loop to be less than 250 ms, if the two procedures are to be called at the start of their respective time slots. This may require the PROC sections to have calls to machine code routines to keep execution time to a minimum, if a large number of tasks are to be included in the time slots available.

A complete example based on this idea is now developed. It is kept simple by including only one routine to be executed four times per second. The BASIC program is almost identical to that already described but the fast routine which makes use of the user port is written in assembly code.

The procedure PROConesec calls PROCqsec as before and has the single function of updating the elapsed time on the display. Any number of additional utilities could be placed in this procedure, as long as the time constraints mentioned earlier are not exceeded.

The procedure PROCqsec calls the assembly code routine, strtst, which is a software implementation of the start-stop relay circuit of many industrial systems. The relay circuit is shown in *Fig. 10.10*.

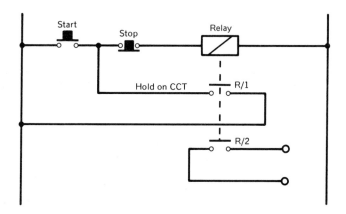

Fig. 10.10. Start/stop relay

The BASIC code of the program is shown in *Fig. 10.11*.

```
100   port=&FE60
110   cntl=&FE62
120   PROCassem
130   @%=&00020108
140   MODE4
150   CALLsetup
160   PROCheading
170   q=0
180   sec=0
190   TIME=0
200   PROConesec
210   oldq=q
220   REPEAT
230     q=(TIME DIV 25) MOD 4
240     sec=TIME DIV 100
250     UNTIL q=(oldq+1) MOD 4
260   IF q=0 THEN PROConesec ELSE PROCqsec
270   GOTO 210
280   END
290   REM****************************
300   DEFPROConesec
310   PROCqsec
320   PRINT TAB(15,4),sec
330   ENDPROC
340   REM****************************
350   DEFPROCqsec
360   CALL strtst
370   ENDPROC
380   REM****************************
390   DEFPROCheading
400   PRINT TAB(0,4)"Elapsed Time:-"
410   ENDPROC
420   REM****************************
```

Fig. 10.11.

Since there are a number of points of difference in this program from that already described, these are now detailed.

The initial section of the program sets up labels for the assembly code program, which is contained in the procedure PROCassem. This procedure is also called at this point to place the machine code instructions in memory.

The two labels are those for the user port and the data direction register. Lines 130 to 190 initialise any variables used in the main program and perform all the functions which are not to be executed within the program loop. The assembly code routine, setup, sets the user port and the procedure, PROCheading, places the fixed text on the screen to prevent wasting time for this function during the time critical part of the program.

The assembly code program contained in the procedure PROC-assem is now listed in *Fig. 10.12*.

110

```
420REM***************************
430 DEFPROCassem
440 FOR z=1 TO 3 STEP 2
450    P%=&1500
460    [OPTz
470    .setup
480    LDA #&F0: STA cntl
490    LDA #&00: STA port
500    RTS
510    .strtst
520    LDA port: STA data
530    AND #&01
540    BNE turnof1
550    JSR chkstr
560    RTS
570    .turnof1
580    LDA data: AND #&BF: STA port
590    RTS
600    .chkstr
610    LDA port: STA data
620    AND #&02
630    BEQ turnon
640    RTS
650    .turnon
660    LDA port: ORA #&40: STA port
670    RTS
680    .data NOP
690    ] NEXT z
700 ENDPROC
```

Fig. 10.12.

As mentioned above this is called at the start of the BASIC program and assembles in two passes since there are forward references in the labels.

The routine, setup, loads the data direction register, labelled cntl, with the value F0 which is 11110000 in binary. This makes the four most significant port bits outputs and the rest inputs. The port is also set up with zero on all output bits. The routine strtst reads the port data and performs the start-stop circuit function shown earlier. The port requires the circuit of *Fig. 10.13* to be connected to it to permit the program to be checked.

There are no loops in the assembly routine but there are a number of alternative paths from the entry point to the point at which control is returned to the main program.

The first check made on entry to the routine is of bit 0 of the port, to which the stop switch is connected. This is checked first, since the output must be turned off as soon as this switch is opened (in practice scanning such a switch four times per second may not be satisfactory). The result of the instruction AND #&01 with the port data will be non-zero if the switch is open so the program branches to the routine turnof1, which turns off the output bit. If the switch is closed the program branches instead to the routine chkstr, which performs

111

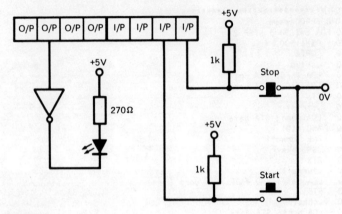

Fig. 10.13.

a similar check on the start switch connected to bit 1. The instruction AND #&02 will produce a zero result if the start switch is closed, and the output will be turned on. When the start switch is open nothing is done and the output is left in its current state. The port data is read and stored at an address labelled data, at the start of the switch checking routine. This ensures that the stop switch is always checked before the output is turned on. The address labelled data is loaded on assembly with a dummy instruction NOP, which is overwritten when any variable data is placed there.

11
File handling

Cassette tapes or discs can be used to store programs and retrieve them for further use. However, it is also possible to use this storage for data which is used by a program. For instance, if you wished to have a telephone directory on computer then all the information could be stored in computer memory or on cassette tape or disc. However, many times the amount of information can be stored on tape or disc compared to computer memory, so maybe only a hundred telephone numbers could be stored in the computer but many thousands on tape. So for programs that need to use or have access to lots of data then 'files' are used. They can also be used to exchange data between programs.

The BBC microcomputer is organised so that both cassette and disc files look the same from a programmer's point of view. This means that you can write and run programs on cassettes and when finance allows the purchase of discs no reprogramming is required. Some commands work only with discs but the majority work with all file systems. Cassette files are not always reliable using 1200 baud speed—300 baud (using *TAPE 3) is safer.

A file is treated as either a file to be written to—an 'out' file, or a file to be read from—an 'in file'. A file has a name, but for speed and ease of program writing a named file is associated with a channel number on the computer. So to begin with we need to inform the computer that we want a file of some file name and wish it to be either an 'in' or an 'out' file. As we don't yet have a file, let's start by going through a program to open an 'out' file and write some data to it.

We start with the command OPENOUT ('file name'). If we are going to call the file 'first' then we should find a line in the program:

    300   channel=OPENOUT ("FIRST")

This will tell the computer that a channel number (it will assign what value it is) is to be an 'out' file with a name FIRST. To send data to that channel we use a PRINT# command, so:

    310   PRINT# channel, 40

would write the number 40 into a file named FIRST. Note that we didn't use the file name in the PRINT command, just the channel number.

When we have finished we need to tell the computer that the file is ended and release the channel number for further use and we use the CLOSE command, so

320   CLOSE# channel

will write an end of file marker to the file and release the channel.

We now have a file called FIRST with a single entry of 40 in it. To read this back into another part of the program or into another program we first need to open it as an 'in' file:

500   channel=OPENIN("FIRST")

This will now assign a channel as in input file and now:

510   INPUT# channel, Data

will read 40 into Data which we could print out or use later. Again we should close a file when we have finished with it, so:

520   CLOSE# channel

will tidy things up.

The program of *Fig. 11.1* is an example to demonstrate the above ideas. It is useful as a test routine as it writes ten random numbers onto the tape or disc and then reads them back and prints them out side by side. If all worked correctly then you should have two columns of ten identical numbers. If this does not occur then you have a problem, either with the volume control on your cassette or with unclean heads on a disc drive.

In this case the writing and reading of the files has been done by procedures. The program first generates ten random numbers and stores them in an array called D. This is then written to tape or disc. Thus you should start a cassette tape with the record button pressed just as you start to run the program. The word DONE is then printed. If you are using a cassette then you should rewind the tape and press play. The program then reads the ten numbers into array R and prints them out. The file is called TRIALFILE and the variable X is used as a channel number.

You can have more than one 'in' file or 'out' file open at the same time but as this uses a lot of memory space try to keep the number as low as possible. Now let us look at some more complex uses of files.

We will consider how to set up a stock control system. In the previous program we knew how many items were on the file, thus when

```
10 DIM D(10),R(10)
20 C=0
30 REPEAT
40   C=C+1
50   D(C)=RND(10)
60 UNTIL C>=10
70 PROCwritefile
75 PRINT"DONE"
80 PROCreadfile
90 C=0
100 REPEAT
110   C=C+1
120   PRINT D(C),R(C)
130 UNTIL C<=10
200 END
300 DEFPROCwritefile
310 LOCAL C
320 C=0
330 X=OPENOUT("TRIALFILE")
340   REPEAT
350     C=C+1
360       PRINT#X,D(C)
370     UNTIL C<=10
380 CLOSE#X
390 ENDPROC
400 DEFPROCreadfile
410 LOCAL C
420 C=0
430 X=OPENIN("TRIALFILE")
440   REPEAT
450     C=C+1
460       INPUT#X,R(C)
470   INPUT#X,R(C)
480 CLOSE#X
490 ENDPROC
```

Fig. 11.1.

reading back to data, we knew when we reached the end of a file. In general, however, we do not know how many items are on the file. There are two ways of ensuring that we know when we are at the end of the file.

1. Place a special character as the last item in the file.
2. Use the EOF function provided with the BBC BASIC.

The program in *Fig. 11.2* places the characters '999' at the end of a test file.

```
100 REM File creation program
110 file_no=OPENOUT("TESTFILE")
120 PRINT#file_no,9,8,20,999
130 CLOSE#file_no
```

Fig. 11.2.

We can now recognise when we reach the end of file by searching for '999', as in *Fig. 11.3*.

```
200 REM File reading program
210 file_no=OPENIN("TESTFILE")
220 REPEAT
230   INPUT#file_no,item
240   PRINT item
250 UNTIL item=999
260 PRINT "END OF FILE REACHED"
270 CLOSE#file_no
280 END
```

Fig. 11.3.

When we run the file reading program, we have the output illustrated in *Fig. 11.4*.

```
RUN
        9
        8
       20
      999
END OF FILE REACHED
```

Fig. 11.4.

We can add in extra data by entering the following line in the file creation program (*Fig. 11.2*).

115   PRINT # file—no, 3, 11, 18

and RUN the new version of the file creation program.

To recover this data we do not need to amend the file reading program, but simply run it again to obtain the output shown in *Fig. 11.5*.

```
        3
       11
       18
        9
        8
       20
      999
END OF FILE REACHED
```

Fig. 11.5.

The other method of recognising the end of file is to use the EOF function, supplied with the system.

The letters of EOF stand for 'end of file' and this function returns a boolean value of true when the end of file has been reached. It is best seen how this works by example. If we assume that the file

116

TESTFILE has been set up with the amended file creation program, then the program in *Fig. 11.6* can be used to recover the stored data:

```
LIST
 200 REM File reading program 2
 210 file_no=OPENIN("TESTFILE")
 220 REPEAT
 230   INPUT#file_no, item
 240   PRINT item
 250 UNTIL EOF#file_no
 260 PRINT "END OF FILE REACHED"
 270 CLOSE#file_no
 280 END
```

Fig. 11.6.

When we run this version of the file reading program, we have the output shown in *Fig. 11.7*.

```
        3
       11
       18
        9
        8
       20
      999
END OF FILE REACHED
```

Fig. 11.7.

All the routines discussed so far could be used on either the cassette operating system or the disc operating system. However, the cassette based system has serious limitations regarding developing commercial software; for example, only one file can be open at a time. It is far better to use the disc operating system for software projects like stock control, financial planning or payroll. In these systems you will want to be able to open more than one file at a time, and also be able to access a file to pick out a particular piece of information without reading the whole file first.

To use the disc operating system, we first of all call it in by using the command

*DISC

Once this has been executed, we can then make use of the full facilities of the BBC file commands.

Stock control systems

In a stock control system, we would wish to be able to do the following:

1. Allow transactions to be entered and verified. A transaction will be either a withdrawal or addition to stock.
2. Allow the stock file to be updated.

Thus we have the system shown in *Fig. 11.8.*

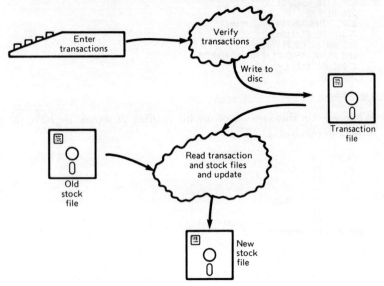

Fig. 11.8.

Suppose the file holds the following information on each item of stock

stock number
a short description
current level of stock

and is arranged in order of stock number, for example, a stock file could contain the following data

1, BBC Model A, 951
3, DISK DRIVES (SINGLE), 951
9, DISK DRIVES (DUAL), 7
etc.

Then, in the transaction file, we would want each record to contain:

stock number
code for withdrawal or addition
quantity withdrawn/added
Let code=1 be withdrawal, code=2 be addition.

118

To make the update program simple, we would arrange this file also to be in stock number sequence.

We now have two programs to write, the first one (*Fig. 11.9*) accepts data from keyboard and does some error checking. The second (*Fig. 11.10*) updates the stock file.

Program 1

```
LIST
    100 REM Transaction validation program
    110 REM This program accepts data from keyboard and writes valid data
            onto the disc, invalid data is displayed onto the screen
    120 REM The transaction record has 3 parts to it : stock-number, code
            and quantity
    130 REM The checks made are
    140 REM     1. Stock numbers are in sequence
    150 REM     2. Code = 1 or 2
    160 REM     3. Quantity is a positive integer
    170 REM Variable initialisation block, f_n is file number
    180 f_n=OPENOUT("VALID_DATA")
    190 stock_number%=99:code%=0:quantity%=0:old_stocknumber%=0
    200 REM We will use stock_number% to terminate data input
    210 REPEAT
    220     CLS : REM clear screen
    230     error_flag=0
    240     REM The following set of code inputs data
    250     INPUT"Enter stock_number (0 to end)"stock_number%
    260     INPUT''"Enter code (1 or 2)"code%
    270     INPUT''"Enter quantity"quantity%
    280     REM The following code verifies data
    290     IF (stock_number%<old_stocknumber% AND stock_number%<>0) THEN
                PRINT "STOCK NUMBER INVALID":error_flag=1
    300     IF NOT (code%=1 OR code%=2) THEN PRINT "CODE INVALID":error_flag=1
    310     IF quantity%<1 THEN PRINT "QUANTITY INVALID":error_flag=1
    320     IF error_flag=0 THEN PRINT#f_n,stock_number%,code%,quantity%:
            old_stocknumber%=stock_number% ELSE PRINT"HIT KEY":KEY=GET
    330 UNTIL stock_number%=0
    340 CLOSE#f_n
    350 END
```

Fig. 11.9.

This program can be used to create a file of transactions on disc. We can now use this data to update a second disc file holding the stock (*Fig. 11.10*).

Thus, in the stock update program we need to have three files open at the one time. Therefore, this program must use the disc operating system.

The program is listed in *Fig. 11.11*.

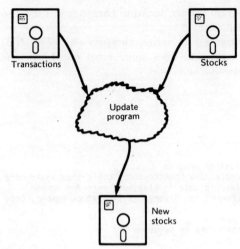

Fig. 11.10.

```
100 REM Stock update program
110 REM This program reads a file of transactions and uses this information
        to update a master stock file.
120 trans=OPENIN("VALID_DATA"):
    REM Transaction file ends with stock_number%=0
130 old_master=OPENIN("OLD_MASTER"):REM This file is sorted in sequence,
    last item is stock_number%=0
140 new_master=OPENOUT("NEW_MASTER"):REM This file will contain new version
    of stock file
150 INPUT#trans,stkno%,code%,quantity%
160 REPEAT
170   INPUT#old_master,stock_number%,description$,current_level%
180   IF stock_number%=stkno% THEN PROCupdate
190   PRINT#new_master,stock_number%description$,current_level%
200 UNTIL stock_number%=0
210 CLOSE#trans
220 CLOSE#old_master
230 CLOSE#new_master
240 END
250 DEF PROCupdate
260 IF code%=1 THEN current_level%=current_level%-quantity% ELSE
    current_level%=current_level%+quantity%
270 INPUT#trans,stkno%,code%,quantity%
280 IF stkno%=stock_number% THEN PROCupdate
290 ENDPROC
```

Fig. 11.11.

120

It would be possible, of course, to write the above program in fewer lines of code, but it is interesting in that it exhibits the use of a recursive procedure. The recursion has been introduced to allow for the case when an individual item of stock has more than one transaction against it.

These two programs were run with the following data (*Fig. 11.12*)

Transactions	Old Stock Data
1,1,2	1,BBC Model A,951
3,2,7	3,Disc Drives (Single),951
9,1,6	9,Disc Drives (Dual),7
0,0,0	11,Printers,9
	0,0,0

Fig. 11.12.

giving the updated stock file in *Fig. 11.13*.

New Stock Data

```
1,BBC Model A,949
3,Disc Drives (Single),958
9,Disc Drives (Dual),1
11,Printers,9
0,0,0
```

Fig. 11.13.

We leave the following programs as an exercise for the reader.

1. A report program to give a printout of stock.
2. An enquiry program, to print out all items of stock with low stock levels.

The type of processing which we have been considering so far is known as sequential processing. It is so called since every item on the files is processed in sequence. With this style of processing we start at the first record and carry on until we reach the last.

It is possible, using the BBC micro DOS, to access a file in a random fashion, but we have to put more effort into the programming. The commands we can use are:

1. BPUT # file-number, byte
2. BGET # file-number, byte
3. PTR # file-number=pointer

BPUT writes a single byte of information onto a file. BGET reads a byte of information from the disc. PTR is a BASIC variable which holds the position of the next byte to be read from a particular file. Since PTR is a variable it can be changed and thus the BBC micro can read a file in a random fashion.

Example of random processing with the BBC micro

Program 1
This program (*Fig. 11.14*) writes a set of 10 records of 2 bytes long made up as follows:

byte 1—Record number (0–255 in decimal)
     2—Contents (1 byte=0–255 in decimal)

```
100 f_n=OPENOUT("TESTFILE")
110 FOR I=1 TO 10
120     BPUT#f_n,I
130     BPUT#f_n,2*I
140 NEXT I
150 CLOSE#f_n
```
Fig. 11.14.

Program 2
This program (*Fig. 11.15*)reads the file TESTFILE sequentially and prints them onto the screen.

```
100 f_n=OPENIN("TESTFILE")
110 FOR I=1 TO 10
120     PRINT BGET#f_n,BGET#f_n
130     PRINT PTR#f_n
140 NEXT I
150 CLOSE#f_n
```
Fig. 11.15.

Program 3
This program (*Fig. 11.16*) allows the user to specify which record he wishes to print onto the screen.

```
100 f_n=OPENIN("TESTFILE")
110 REPEAT
120     INPUT"Which record",record_no
130     PTR#f_n=record_no-1
140 REM the first record is no.0
150     PRINT BGET#f_n,BGET#f_n
160     INPUT"PRESS 'C' TO CONTINUE"response$
170 UNTIL response$<>"C"
180 CLOSE#f_n
```
Fig. 11.16.

Thus it can be seen that if you wish to use random processing, you must fully understand the structure of your file. It is possible using these features of BBC BASIC to construct rather complex software for file handling.

122

12
Hardware

After the brief description given in the Introduction, this chapter presents a more detailed examination of the hardware. The BBC micro is sold in two forms, the model A basic 16K machine and the model B extended 32K machine. However, a variety of internal and external options could lead to several hundred versions of the machine. It follows that some of the features described in this chapter may not be implemented on your computer.

General

All the chips are held on a single printed circuit board (*Fig. 12.1*).

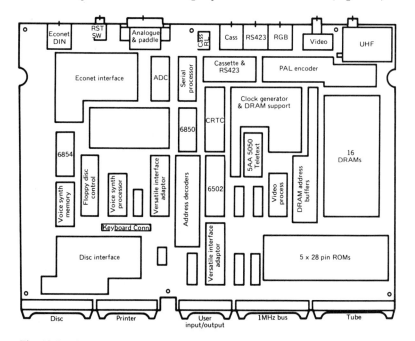

Fig. 12.1. Board layout

The layout is well planned from a user standpoint. The back edge of the board can carry up to seven sockets, namely UHF, video out, RGB, RS423, cassette, analogue and ECONET. At the front, edge connectors are accessible from under the machine. These form interfaces for disc, Centronic type printer, user port, 1 MHz bus and the Tube (2 MHz bus).

At the heart of the board is a 6502A microprocessor running at either 1 MHz or 2 MHz. Normally the processor runs at the higher speed but slows down to talk to slow devices such as the analogue to digital converter (ADC), the versatile interface adaptor (VIA), and the 1 MHz extension bus.

The random access memory (RAM) is provided by either eight or sixteen 4816A (16K×1 bit) dynamic memory chips. The 16K (ROM type 23128) machine operating system takes care of all housekeeping duties, scanning the keyboard, driving the display, etc. One kilobyte of this ROM is left unused and it is into this area of the system memory map that the various input/output devices are placed. (Note: on early versions of the machine the operating system was contained within four 4K byte EPROMS. This was a temporary solution by the manufacturer to avoid the expense of producing a

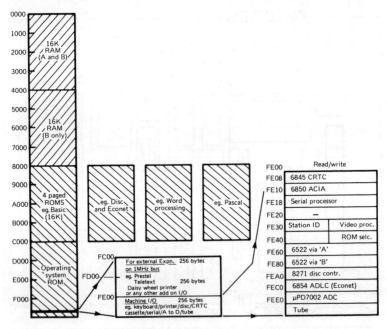

Fig. 12.2. BBC micro memory map

124

16K byte mask programmed ROM until the operating system was completely developed.) Alongside the operating system ROM are four other sockets capable of holding 16K byte devices. Normally one will hold the BASIC interpreter but other options include PASCAL, DISC operating system and ECONET communication software. All these devices occupy the same space in the system memory map and selection is achieved under software control. There are no defined sockets for these options. Each ROM contains an identification code which is used by the operating system to locate the desired chip. Once found, it is activated by the ROM select latch (IC76).

The memory map of the BBC micro is shown in *Fig. 12.2.*

Keyboard/speech-music generators

A 6522 versatile interface adaptor chip (IC9), dedicated to internal system use, acts as an interface between the microprocessor and the following devices:

—keyboard
—sound generator
—speech generator
—ROM pack adaptor
—display mode selection.

The VIA is a complex device containing two parallel ports with associated control lines, two counter timers and a serial to parallel shift register. A detailed description of its operation would easily fill this chapter. However, *Fig. 12.3* summarises the function of each of its internal registers.

Part of Port B drives an addressable latch (IC32) which in turn selects one of the devices. This latch also controls the amount of RAM devoted to the display, i.e. either 1K, 8K, 10K or 20K. Port A forms a 'slow data bus', transferring information between the processor and the selected device.

The keyboard switches are arranged in rows and columns forming a matrix. If any key is depressed a signal is sent to control line CA2 on the VIA which in turn interrupts the microprocessor. To discover which key was pressed, the processor then enters a software scanning routine which searches the rows and columns looking for the depressed key.

Voice synthesis is possible using the Texas Instruments chips TMS 5220 (IC99) and TMS 6100 (IC98). The latter is a memory device containing 'canned' speech. A four channel sound generator chip 76489 (IC18) can be programmed to give varying frequency and

Address	Adressed register	Write	Read	Notes
0	Port B	Write ORB Clear CB2 and CB1 Interrupt Flags (IFR3 and IFR4)	Read IRB Clear CB2 and CB1 Interrupt Flags (IFR3 and IFR4)	1 = High, 0 = Low
1	Port A	Write ORA Clear CA2 and CA1 Interrupt Flags (IFR0 and IFR1)	Read IRA Clear CA2 and CA1 Interrupt Flags (IFR0 and IFR1)	1 = High, 0 = Low Controls CA2 Handshake
2	Direction B	Write DDRB	Read DDRB	0 = Input, 1 = Output
3	Direction A	Write DDRA	Read DDRA	0 = Input, 1 = Output
4	Timer 1	Write T1L-L	Read T1C-L Clear T1 Interrupt Flag (IFR6)	
5	Timer 1	Write T1L-H & T1C-H Transfer T1L-L to T1C-L Clear T1 Interrupt Flag (IFR6) Initiate T1 Counting	Read T1C-H	
6	Timer 1	Write T1L-L	Read T1L-L	
7	Timer 1	Write T1L-H Clear T1 Interrupt Flag (IFR6)	Read T1L-H	
8	Timer 2	Write T2L-L	Read T2C-L Clear T2 Interrupt Flag (IFR5)	
9	Timer 2	Write T2C-H Transfer T2L-L to T2C-L Clear T2 Interrupt Flag (IFR5) Initiate T2 Counting	Read T2C-H	
A	SR	Write SR Clear SR Interrupt Flag (IFR2)	Read SR Clear SR Interrupt Flag (IFR2)	
B	ACR	Write ACR	Read ACR	
C	PCR	Write PCR	Read PCR	
D	IFR	Write IFR	Read IFR	1 = Detected 0 = Not detected
E	IER	Write IER	Read IER	1 = Enable, 0 = Disable
F	IRA/ORA	Write ORA Clear CA2 and CA1 Interrupt Flags (IFR0 and IFR1)	Read IRA Clear CA2 and CA1 Interrupt Flags (IFR0 and IFR1)	1 = High, 0 = Low No effect on CA2 Handshake

Fig. 12.3. VIA internal registers

attenuation on each channel. It is possible to mix the voice and music signals together with an external analogue signal, input from the 1 MHz extension bus, before final amplification by the power amplifier LM386 (IC19).

Finally, Port B pins 4 and 5 are programmed as inputs and act as 'fire button' signals when used together with games paddles connected to the analogue input.

Parallel printer and user ports

Port A of a second VIA (IC69) drives an octal buffer, 74LS244 (IC70), to provide a Centronics standard parallel printer interface. Port B is left free to allow users to interface their own applications to the computer.

126

Display

Two integrated circuits lie at the heart of the machine's memory mapped display.

—Motorola 6845 cathode ray tube controller (IC2)
—Video processor—an uncommitted logic array (ULA) designed by Acorn (IC8)

The CRTC chip generates the synchronisation signals required by the video display, together with all the addresses necessary to scan through the screen memory, updating the display. Further, the design of the address circuitry ensures that the sequence of addresses generated by the CRTC chip can also be used to refresh the dynamic

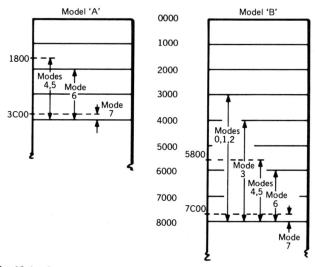

Fig. 12.4.   Screen memory

RAM. Every clock cycle (500 ns) control of the memory is switched between the microprocessor and the CRTC chip, allowing the former access to update the screen memory, and the latter access to deliver the contents of the memory to the video processor. This device serialises the byte into one bit stream of 8 bits or two bit streams of 4 bits, etc., providing display modes varying from 640 pixels in two colours to 160 pixels in eight colours. The video processor also contains some high speed static RAM known as the PALETTE. This memory can be programmed from the microprocessor and is used to define the relationship between the logical colour information contained in the system memory and the actual colour which

127

appears on the screen. A command which would normally produce, say, yellow text can have the PALETTE programmed to give a final display in, say, red. (VDU 19 and VDU 20 affect the palette.) In display modes 0 to 6 characters are generated by software routines. Mode 7 uses an SAA 5050 (IC5) character generator chip to create the teletext character set.

The position and size of the memory used for display in each of the eight graphics modes is given in *Fig. 12.4.*

A to D converter

A NEC NPD 7002 (IC73) four channel analogue to digital converter is connected directly to the computer's data bus. Each channel has a resolution of 12 bits. The end of conversion signal is connected to CB1 of the system VIA (IC8) which in turn interrupts the processor initiating a routine to update the current stored value of each channel. Samples are taken every 10 ms, resulting in all four channels being updated every 40 ms. A series of three diodes provides a reference voltage of roughly 1.8 V.

Serial and cassette interface

Serial data from devices such as CRT terminals, modems, cassette recorders, etc., is interfaced to the microprocessor using a Motorola 6850 asynchronous communications interface adaptor (IC4). A second ULA device (IC7), known as the serial processor, contains a programmable baud rate generator together with the circuitry

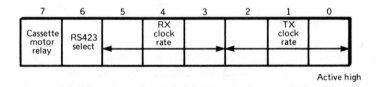

Bit 7   operates the cassette motor ('I'on/'0'off)

Bit 6   selects the RS423 or cassette ('I'RS423/'0'cassette)

Bits 5,4,3 - set the baud rate clock for receiving serial data

bits 2,1,0 - set the baud rate clock for transmitting serial data.

Fig. 12.5.   ULA control register

required to interface the ACIA to an audio cassette. The ULA is configured through a control register at &FE10.

The 6850 (ACIA) occupies two memory locations in the system memory map:

Address	*Function*	
	Write operation	*Read operation*
&FE08	Control Register	Status Register
&FE09	Transmit Data Register	Receive Data Register

During a WRITE operation &FE08 acts as a CONTROL register configuring the 6850 (see *Fig. 12.6*).

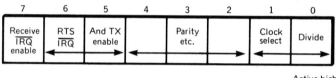

Active high

Bit 7	"I" enables interrupts for received characters
Bits 5,6	Control interrupts on transmit and RTS output
Bits 4,3,2	Set word length, parity and stop bits
Bits 1,0	Divide, select and master reset

Fig. 12.6. &FE08 as a control register

During a READ operation &FE08 acts as a STATUS register reporting its current state (see *Fig. 12.7*, next page).

Further details on the operation of the 6850 can be obtained from Motorola's own publication 'Microcomputer Components'.

Disc drive controller

The control circuitry required to drive one or two single or double sided 5¼ in or 8 in floppy disc drives is included on the main printed circuit board. An Intel 8271 (IC78) controller chip handles the data, and provides all the control signals required by the disc drive.

7	6	5	4	3	2	1	0
$\overline{\text{IRQ}}$	Parity error	Overrun	Framing error	Clear to send	DCD	TX empty	RX full

Active high

Bit 7   Indicates the state of the $\overline{\text{IRQ}}$ output

Bit 6   Parity error flag

Bit 5   Overrun error flag

Bit 4   Framing error flag

Bit 3   Indicates the state of the clear to send $\overline{\text{(CTS)}}$ input

Bit 2   Data carrier detect bit

Bit 1   Transmit data register empty flag

Bit 0   Receive data register full flag

Fig. 12.7.   &FE08 as a status register

ECONET Network

The ECONET network is based on the Motorola 6854 advanced data link controller chip (IC89). Data is transferred between stations in a serial format at transmission rates of the order of 210 kilobaud. Each station of the ECONET has a station identity set by the links on S11. Stations on the network are connected by a four core twisted pair cable.

1 MHz bus and tube

The 1 MHz bus provides a means of interfacing various peripheral or I/O devices to the processor. Address lines A0 to A7 and data lines D0 to D7 are provided after buffering by IC71 and IC72. Two page select signals JIM &$\overline{\text{FD00}}$ and FRED &$\overline{\text{FC00}}$ are also provided. These two signals define the only free memory space in the expanded (32K RAM) machine.

The tube provides selected address and data bus lines direct from the internal system bus. This interface has been designed to drive the second language processor option containing another microprocessor with extra RAM.

130

RAM Expansion

8 off 4816AP-3 dynamic RAM's

IC's 61 to 68

Link S25 moved to NORTH position

Centronics Printer Interface – User Port

1 off 6522 VIA (IC69)

1 off 74LS244 (IC70)

Printer connector PL9 – 26 way insulation displacement connector (IDC)

User I/O connector PL10 – 20 way IDC

A to D Converter – Analogue Input

1 off NPD 7002 ADC (IC73)
1 off 74LS00 (IC77)
Analogue input connector – 15 way D type (SK6)

Tube

1 off 40 way IDC PL12

1 MHz Bus

1 off 74LS244 (IC71)

1 off 74LS245 (IC72)

1 off 34 way IDC, PL11

RS423

1 off 88LS120 IC74

1 off 3691 IC75

1 off 5 pin DIN SK4

ROM Paging

1 off 74LS163 (IC76)

Disk Connector

1 off 34 way IDC PL8

RGB Monitor

1 off 6 pin DIN SK3

Fig. 12.8. Components required for expansion to model B

Expanding the model A

Acorn's dealer network will undertake the necessary work to expand a model A machine to a model B. For those with some technical skill this expansion is relatively simple, involving soldering edge connectors to the board and inserting integrated circuits into holders already present. However, bear in mind that any cost advantage gained may be at the expense of a loss of your guarantee.

Fig. 12.8 shows the components required to obtain each of the extra features provided by the model B machine.

Appendix A
BBC microcomputer specification

Part 1—Firmware specification
The BASIC language interpreter

The BASIC interpreter works through one of three filing systems: a cassette filing system (CFS), a disc filing system (DFS) or a network filing system (NFS). The user can move between filing systems and can pass commands direct to the filing system.

The BASIC interpreter contains an Assembler which accepts standard 6502 mnemonics.

Variables: Variable names may be of unlimited length and all characters are significant. Variable names must start with a letter. They can only contain the characters A..Z, a..z, 0..9 and underline. Embedded keywords are allowed. Upper and lower case variables of the same name are different.

Keywords are recognised before anything else. Pseudo variables act as variables in that if PI is a (pseudo-) variable it does not affect PILE.

The following types of variable are allowed:
A   real numeric
A%   integer numeric
A$ string

The 'static' variables @% and A%..Z% are regarded as special in that they are not cleared by the commands or statements RUN, CHAIN and CLEAR. In addition A%, C%, X% and Y% have special uses in CALL and USR routines and P% has a special meaning in the assembler. The special variable @% controls numeric print formatting.

Real variables have a range of approximately $+-1E-38$ to $+-1E38$ and numeric functions evaluate to nine

133

significant figure accuracy. Internally every real number is stored in 40 bits.

Integer variables are stored in 32 bits and have a range of about +−2E9.

String variables may contain up to 255 characters.

All arrays must be dimensioned before use.
All statements can also be used as direct commands.

BBC BASIC keywords

ABS	A function giving the absolute value of its argument.
ACS	A function giving the arc cosine of its argument in radians.
ADVAL	A function which returns the last known value of ADC channel n.
AND	The operation of integer bitwise logical AND between two items.
ASC	A function returning the ASCII character value of the first character of the argument string. If the string is null then −1 will be returned.
ASN	A function giving the arc sine of its argument in radians.
ATN	A function giving the arc tangent of its argument in radians.
AUTO	A command allowing the user to enter lines without first typing in the number of the line. AUTO mode is left with <escape>. Step size range is 1 to 255.
BGET	A function which gets a byte from the file whose channel number is its argument.
BPUT	A statement which puts a byte to the file whose channel number is the first argument. The second argument's least significant byte is sent.
CHAIN	A statement which will load and run the program whose name is specified in the argument.
CHR$	A string function whose value is a string of length 1 containing the ASCII character specified by the least significant byte of the numeric argument.
CLEAR	A statement which clears all the dynamically declared variables, including strings.
CLOSE	A statement used to close a sequential file. CLOSE 0 will close all sequential files.

CLG	A statement which clears the graphics area on the VDU to the current graphics background colour and moves the graphics pointer to 0,0 (bottom left).
CLS	A statement which clears the text area on the VDU to the current text background colour and moves the cursor to 0,0 (top left).
COLOUR	A statement which sets the text foreground and background colours of the 'soft' displays (modes 0–6).
COS	A function giving the cosine of its radian argument.
COUNT	A function returning the number of characters printed since the last new line.
DATA	A program object which must precede all lists of data for READ.
DEG	A function which converts radians to degrees.
DEF	A program object which must precede declaration of a user function FN or a user procedure PROC.
DELETE	A command which deletes a group of lines from the program. Both start and end lines of the group will be deleted.
DIV	A binary operation giving the integer quotient of two items.
DRAW	Draws a line to the specified position in the current graphics foreground colour.
ELSE	A statement delimiter which behaves as follows: When encountered as a delimiter the rest of the line is ignored. If in an IF statement the Boolean is false, the statements after ELSE will be executed.
END	A statement causing the interpreter to return to direct mode.
ENDPROC	A statement denoting the end of a procedure.
ENVELOPE	A statement taking 14 parameters which are bytes. The bytes are passed to the machine operating system to control the sound generator.
EOF	A function which will return −1 (TRUE) if the file whose channel number is the argument is at its end.
EOR	The operation of bitwise integer logical EXCLUSIVE-OR between two items as 32 bit integers.
ERL	A function returning the line number of the line where the last error occurred.
ERR	A function returning the error code number of the last error which occurred.
EVAL	A function which applies the interpreter's expression evaluation program to the characters held in the argument string.

EXP	A function returning e to the power of the argument.
EXT	A function which returns the length, in bytes, of the file whose channel number is the argument.
FALSE	A function returning 0, i.e. false.
FN	A reserved word used at the start of all user declared functions.
FOR	A statement initialising a FOR . . . NEXT loop.
GCOL	A statement to set the graphics foreground and background colours and actions.
GET	A function and compatible string function that reads the next character from the input stream, usually the keyboard.
GOTO	A statement which will go to a line with constant number of calculated value.
GOSUB	As GOTO but allows RETURN.
HIMEM	A pseudo-variable which sets and gives the maximum address used by the interpreter.
IF	A statement which sets up a test condition, which can be used to control the subsequent action of the computer.
INKEY	A function and compatible string function that will do a GET/GET$, waiting for a maximum of n clock ticks (usually 10 ms each). If no key is pressed in the time limit, INKEY will return −1 and INKEY$ will return a null string.
INPUT	A statement to input values from the current input stream (usually keyboard).
INPUT LINE	A statement of identical syntax to INPUT which uses a new line for each item to be input.
INPUT #	A statement which reads data in internal format from a file and puts them in the specified variables.
INSTR	A function which returns the position of a substring within a string, optionally starting the search at a specified place in the string. If the substring is not found, 0 is returned.
INT	A function truncating a real number to the lower integer.
LEFT$	A string function which returns the left n characters of the string.
LEN	A function which returns the length of the argument string.
LET	Optional assignment statement.
LIST	A command which causes lines of the current program to be listed out with the automatic formatting options specified by LISTO.

LISTO	A command which sets options for formatting a LISTed program.
LN	A function giving the natural logarithm of its argument.
LOAD	A command which loads a new program from a file and CLEARs the variables of the old program.
LOCAL	A statement to declare variables for local use inside a function (FN) or procedure (PROC). LOCAL saves the values of its arguments in such a way that they will be restored at=or ENDPROC.
LOG	A function giving the base-10 logarithm of its argument.
LOMEM	A pseudo-variable which controls where in memory the dynamic data structures are to be placed.
MID$	A string function which returns N characters of the string starting from character M.
MOD	A binary operation giving the signed remainder of the integer division.
MODE	A statement which will select the specified VDU screen mode (0–7).
MOVE	A statement which moves the graphics pointer to the specified position.
NEW	A command which initialises the interpreter for a new program to be typed in.
NEXT	The statement delimiting FOR . . . NEXT loops.
NOT	A unary operator equivalent to unary minus.
OLD	A command which undoes the effect of NEW provided no new lines have been typed in and no variables have been created.
ON	A statement which causes a program jump to one of a number of locations depending on the value of a defined variable.
OPENIN	A function which returns the channel number of the file. The file is opened for input and updating.
OPENOUT	A function which returns the channel number of a file with optional creation of the file.
OPT	An assembler pseudo operation controlling the method of assembly.
OR	The operation of bitwise integer logical OR between two items.
PAGE	A pseudo-variable controlling the starting address of the current text area.
PI	A function returning 3.14159265.
PLOT	A statement controlling most of the graphics. The

	first argument controls whether points or lines will be drawn, how pixels are put on the screen, and whether the coordinates (the other arguments) are relative or absolute.
POINT	A function returning the colour of the point on the screen or −1 if off screen.
POS	A function returning the horizontal position of the cursor on the screen; left hand column is 0.
PRINT	A statement which 'prints' a specified message on the screen.
PRINT #	A statement which writes the internal form of a value out to a sequential file.
PROC	A reserved word used at the start of all user declared numeric procedures.
PTR #	A statement and function which allows the programmer to move a pointer to a serial file and thus enables random access.
RAD	A function which converts degrees to radians.
READ	A statement which will assign to variables values read from the DATA statements in the program.
REM	A statement that causes the rest of the line to be ignored.
RENUMBER	A command which will renumber the lines and correct the cross references inside a program.
REPEAT	A statement which is the starting point of a REPEAT . . . UNTIL loop.
REPORT	A statement which prints out a new line followed by the error string associated with the last error which occurred.
RESTORE	RESTORE can be used at any time in a program to set the place where DATA comes from.
RETURN	A statement causing a return to the statement after the most recent GOSUB statement.
RIGHT$	A string function which returns the right n characters of the string. If there are insufficient characters in the string then all are returned.
RND	A function with optional parameter. RND(1) returns a real number in the range 0.0 to .99999999. RND returns a random integer 0—&FFFFFFFF. RND(n) returns an integer in the range 1 to n.
RUN	Start execution of the program.
SAVE	A statement which saves the current program area to a file.
SGN	A function returning −1 for negative argument, 0 for

	0 argument and +1 for positive argument.
SIN	A function giving the sine of its radian argument.
SOUND	A statement which instructs the computer to generate a sound. The accompanying parameters determine amplitude, envelope, frequency (or period), duration.
SPC	A function which, when used with PRINT or INPUT statements causes a specified number of spaces to be printed.
SQR	A function returning the square root of its argument.
STEP	This function specifies step sizes other than 1 when used as part of the FOR . . .NEXT loop.
STOP	STOP causes the execution of the program to stop and prints a message to this effect.
STR$	A string function which converts a number into the equivalent string representation.
STRING$	A function which produces a long string consisting of multiple copies of a shorter string.
TAB	This function is used with PRINT and INPUT and has two versions: TAB(X) prints spaces (and new line if necessary) to reach the specified column; TAB(X,Y) moves the cursor directly to the specified coordinates.
TAN	A function giving the tangent of its radian argument.
THEN	A keyword used with IF to decide on a course of action.
TIME	A pseudo-variable which reads and sets the lower four bytes of the computational elapsed time clock.
TOP	A function which returns the value of the first free location after the end of the current text.
TO	Part of the FOR . . . TO . . . STEP statement.
TRACE	TRACE ON causes the interpreter to print executed line numbers when it encounters them.
TRUE	A function having a true value (-1).
UNTIL	A part of the REPEAT . . . UNTIL structure.
USR	A function allowing machine code to return a value directly for things which do not require the flexibility of CALL.
VAL	A function which converts a character string representing a number into numeric form.
VDU	A statement which takes a list of numeric arguments and sends them to OSWRCH.

VPOS   A function returning the vertical cursor position.
WIDTH   A statement controlling output overall field width.

Part 11—Hardware specification

Case

Dimensions: 400 mm wide by 400 mm deep by 60 mm high approx.
Material: Injection moulded thermoplastic.

Electrical safety

The unit meets the appropriate BEAB, BSI and European stan-
dards. It is constructed in accordance with BSI Class 1 requirements, i.e. all exposed metalwork is connected to earth via the earth
lead of the three-core mains cable. All points which could be at
mains potential when power is applied are inaccessible to the 'standard finger'.

Keyboard

The keyboard is in standard QWERTY format using a pitch
between keys and between rows of 19 mm (0.75 in), with a conventional row-stagger of 9.5 mm (0.375 in) and 4.76 mm (0.1875 in).
There are four rows of alphanumeric keys plus a space-bar and an
additional top row of ten software-definable keys and a break key, 74
keys in all.

The keys have positive action with a total travel of approximately
5 mm (0.2 in), the keypress being detected at approximately 50%
total travel.

The keyboard has two-key rollover on all keys except SHIFT,
CTRL, SHIFT LOCK and CAPS LOCK.

Power supply

The power supply accepts a mains input of between 220 and 260 V
rms at a frequency of 47–63 Hz. The total consumption should not
exceed 50 VA. The output voltages are +5 V, +12 V and −5 V
with current capacities 3.75 A, 1.25 and 0.1 A respectively. The
power supply is protected against overload and will protect itself
from damage through overheating. A high quality square pin mains
plug with a 3 A fuse is supplied ready fitted.

Composite video output

A 1 V pk-pk (75 ohms) composite video (PAL coded) output is provided on a 75 ohm BNC socket accessible at the rear of the machine. The socket is not fitted in the model A machine but all circuitry associated with the video output is included as standard. The TV standard is 625 lines, 50-field interlaced, PAL, with a field-sync pulse consisting of a single broad pulse of 128 s duration. The PAL subcarrier need not be linelocked but must be in the range 4.43361875 MHz +/− 100 Hz over the temperature range 5–35°C (ambient). The signal is capable of being displayed in colour on a typical PAL (baseband input) monitor and of being recorded and replayed in colour on an appropriate video cassette recorder (VHS, Beta, VR2000 and U-Matic formats).

UHF output

The UHF output is from an Astec modulator fixed tuned to approximately channel 36, for feeding to a domestic TV set. This is negatively modulated by a video signal as defined in the previous section, and is capable of being displayed in colour on a typical domestic receiver. A flying lead is provided, terminated by a standard Belling-Lee plug, at least 2 m in length.

RGB outputs

Four outputs at TTL levels are provided, being red, green and blue video signals and a composite (mixed) sync pulse signal. These are suitable for driving a high input impedance RGB monitor. The TV standard will be as previously defined. The connector for these outputs may not be fitted in the model A machine.

Audio cassette interface

A cassette modem is incorporated to allow storage of programs and data on a standard audio cassette recorder, mono or stereo. The format is asynchronous serial data with one start bit (space), eight data bits (LSB first) and a minimum of one stop bit (mark) per byte at one of two alternative speeds, 300 baud and 1200 baud. In the low-speed mode a MARK bit (logic 1) is encoded as 8 cycles of 2400 Hz tone and a SPACE (LOGIC 0) as 4 cycles of 1200 Hz tone. In high-speed mode a MARK is 2 cycles of 2400 Hz and a SPACE is 1 cycle of 1200 Hz tone. It is possible to switch between low-speed (CUTS) mode and high-speed mode under software control, without internal modification.

The demodulator is insensitive to input level variations of up to +6 dB or −12 dB and recovers the UAR/T clock from the tape in order to track short and long-term speed variations. It can cater for an instantaneous speed error of at least 10% WITHOUT relying on the inherent insensitivity to speed of asynchronous data, i.e. bit-centre sampling is maintained. The demodulator is insensitive to the phase of the played-back signal.

Input and output levels are standard DIN. Low-pass filtering is incorporated in the output to avoid subjecting the cassette recorder to high-frequency components which could cause overloading or other forms of distortion. The input circuitry incorporates bandpass filtering to reduce the sensitivity of the demodulator to high and low frequency noise, hum, etc.

The cassette connector is a seven-pin DIN socket wired so that if a stereo recorder is used both channels are recorded, but replay is from the left channel only. A DIN to DIN connecting lead is supplied.

RS423 serial interface

When the cassette interface is not in use, the serial port is available to provide a bi-directional RS423 (+/−5 V) interface for driving a serial printer, etc. Provision is made on the main PCB to include the necessary interface i.c.s, but these are not fitted in the model A machine. Baud rate is selectable under software control to any value from the group 75, 150, 300, 1200, 2400, 4800, 9600 or 19200 bauds; the speeds are accurate to within 0.2%. A simple handshaking input is provided which inhibits the serial output when negative and enables it when positive (RS423 levels).

The RS423 connector is a six-pin DIN type and a suitable adaptor lead to a 25-way D-type socket must be constructed to implement the RS423 option. It may be necessary to have more than one variety of adaptor lead to suit various types of printer. In the standard version the following pins on the D-type are wired: 2—serial input, 3—serial output, 7—signal ground, 20—handshake. In addition pin 6 is wired to a single-bit RS423-level output, capable of being set high or low under software control, which is normally held high (+5 V).

Parallel printer interface

A parallel printer output to Centronics specifications is provided in the model B microcomputer, using a 6522 input/output device plus buffers.

It is possible for the user to intercept the normal driver software for the parallel printer so as to add special features such as software form-feed.

Floppy disc interface

Provision is made on the main PCB to fit a floppy disc controller plus data separator and buffer devices to allow interfacing to one or two mini-floppy or 200 mm (8 in) floppy drives. Neither these devices nor the connector are fitted in the model A machine.

The disc connector is a 34-way type to SA400 specification, but all control signals are present to allow an SA800 specification interface to be implemented by means of an adaptor cable. A link on the main PCB selects the appropriate data rate, i.e. 125 kbits/s for mini-floppy and 250 kbits/s for 200 mm (8 in) floppy. Both hardware and software are capable of supporting 200 mm (8 in) discs to the IBM 3740 specification, although this necessitates fitting an additional ROM which is not present in the basic machine (model A or model B). There is no facility for double-data-density operation.

Analogue inputs

Provision is made on the main PCB to fit a four-channel twelve-bit analogue-to-digital converter device to which external X-Y joystick controls can be connected. The ADC and connector are not fitted in the model A machine. The connector is a 15-way D-type and is common with the light-pen input.

Econet interface

Provision is made on the main PCB to fit a 6845 I/O device plus buffering to implement a standard Econet interface. These devices are not fitted in the model A or the model B machine.

Processor bus interface ('tube')

Unbuffered address, data and control signals are available on a 40-way connector to provide a high-speed interface to an external language processor (e.g. the Z80 CP/M option). The interface is suitable only for this purpose and uses a short length of ribbon cable as interconnection between the two units. The connector is not fitted in the model A machine.

Teletext receiver interface

A buffered processor bus interface is provided for connection to the teletext receiver/data grabber. Interconnection between the main machine and the teletext receiver is by means of ribbon cable having alternate ground conductors, allowing a cable length of at least 30 cm. The connector is fitted as standard in the basic machine, but when adding the teletext receiver option it is necessary to fit two buffer i.c.s and a read-only memory device containing the teletext and telesoftware firmware.

Sound generator

A loudspeaker is fitted as standard. This is fed from a three-voice sound-generator device capable of producing tones and music under software control.

Elapsed time clock

An elapsed-time clock is included, having a resolution of 10 ms. It is possible to set and read the clock time under software control.

User input/output

A TTL-compatible eight-bit port plus two control bits are provided in the model B machine for user input/output.

Start-up options

A set of internal links define the input, output and storage channels, and the screen display option to be used on machine start-up.

Light-pen input

An input is provided which allows the connection of a simple light-pen, fed to the 6845 CRT controller. This input uses the same connector as the analogue inputs. The light pen itself is not supplied.

VDU screen formats

There are eight selectable display formats as follows (RAM requirements in bytes are shown in brackets):

0.	640*256 2-colour graphics & 80*32 text.	(20K)
1.	320*256 4-colour graphics & 40*32 text.	(20K)
2.	160*256 16-colour graphics and 20*32 text.	(20K)
3.	80*25 2-colour text.	(16K)
4.	320*256 2-colour graphics & 40*32 text.	(10K)
5.	160*256 4-colour graphics & 20*32 text.	(10K)
6.	40*25 2-colour text.	(8K)
7.	40*25 teletext-compatible display.	(1K)

Central processor

The CPU is a 6502A running at a 2 MHz clock rate except when accessing some input-output devices, when the effective clock frequency is reduced to 1 MHz.

Memory

The model A machine is equipped with 16 Kbytes dynamic random-access-memory (5 V type), 15 Kbytes operating system ROM (character generator, input/output handlers, cassette operating system, etc.) and 16 Kbytes language ROM (BASIC interpreter). The RAM is capable of expansion to 32 Kbytes and the ROM to 80 Kbytes (being another 16 Kbyte language ROM—e.g. Pascal—plus up to 32 Kbytes of ROM/EPROM containing applications software, etc. Only one of the language ROMs, or the ROM/EPROM, can be enabled at any given time under software control). The model B machine has 32 Kbytes dynamic random access memory.

Expansion

The following additional features are or will shortly be available:
Teletext adaptor
Prestel adaptor
Single-drive 100 Kbyte disk store
Dual-drive 800 Kbyte disk store
6502 second processor expansion
Z80 second processor expansion
CP/M-compatible disk system.

Appendix B

Error messages and error codes

Direct mode only (error code 0):

Silly!

RENUMBER space

LINE space

Disastrous and untrappable:

Bad program

No room

Trappable:

1	Out of range	2	Byte
3	Index	4	Mistake
5	Missing ,	6	Type mismatch
7	No FN	8	$ range
9	Missing "	10	Bad DIM
11	DIM space	12	Not LOCAL
13	No PROC	14	Array
15	Subscript	16	Syntax error
17	Escape	18	Division by zero
19	String too long	20	Too big
21	-ve root	22	Log range
23	Accuracy lost	24	Exp range
25	Bad MODE	26	No such variable
27	Missing)	28	Bad hex
29	No such FN/PROC	30	Bad call
31	Arguments	32	No FOR
33	Can't match FOR	34	FOR variable
35	Too many FORs	36	No TO
37	Too many GOSUBs	38	No GOSUB
39	ON syntax	40	ON range
41	No such line	42	Out of DATA
43	No REPEAT	44	Too many REPEATs

Appendix C
ASCII codes

Decimal Code	Standard Name	Decimal Code	Standard Name	Decimal Code	Standard Name
32	SPACE	64	@	96	
33	!	65	A	97	a
34	"	66	B	98	b
35	#	67	C	99	c
36	$	68	D	1Ø0	d
37	%	69	E	1Ø1	e
38	&	7Ø	F	1Ø2	f
39	'	71	G	1Ø3	g
4Ø	(	72	H	1Ø4	h
41	)	73	I	1Ø5	i
42	*	74	J	1Ø6	j
43	+	75	K	1Ø7	k
44	,	76	L	1Ø8	l
45	−	77	M	1Ø9	m
46	.	78	N	11Ø	n
47	/	79	O	111	o
48	Ø	8Ø	P	112	p
49	1	81	Q	113	q
5Ø	2	82	R	114	r
51	3	83	S	115	s
52	4	84	T	116	t
53	5	85	U	117	u
54	6	86	V	118	v
55	7	87	W	119	w
56	8	88	X	12Ø	x
57	9	89	Y	121	y
58	:	9Ø	Z	122	z
59	;	91	[	123	{
6Ø	<	92	/	124		
61	=	93	]	125	}
62	>	94	^	126	~
63	?	95	—	127	DEL

Appendix D
6502 instruction set

Add memory to accumulator with carry **ADC**

Operation: A+M+C—A, C

N Z C I D V
/ / / - - /

Addressing mode	Assembly language form		OP Code	No. Bytes	No. Cycles
Immediate	ADC	#Oper	69	2	2
Zero Page	ADC	Oper	65	2	3
Zero Page, X	ADC	Oper, X	75	2	4
Absolute	ADC	Oper	6D	3	4
Absolute, X	ADC	Oper, X	7D	3	4*
Absolute, Y	ADC	Oper, Y	79	3	4*
(Indirect, X)	ADC	(Oper, X)	61	2	6
(Indirect), Y	ADC	(Oper), Y	71	2	5*

* Add 1 if page boundary is crossed.

AND memory with accumulator **AND**

Operation: A∧M—A

N Z C I D V
/ / - - - -

Addressing mode	Assembly language form		OP Code	No. Bytes	No. Cycles
Immediate	AND	#Oper	29	2	2
Zero Page	AND	Oper	25	2	3
Zero Page, X	AND	Oper, X	35	2	4
Absolute	AND	Oper	2D	3	4
Absolute, X	AND	Oper, X	3D	3	4*
Absolute, Y	AND	Oper, Y	39	3	4*
(Indirect, X)	AND	(Oper, X)	21	2	6
(Indirect), Y	AND	(Oper), Y	31	2	5*

* Add 1 if page boundary is crossed.

148

ASL
Shift Left One Bit (Memory or Accumulator)
Operation: C—76543210—0

$$N\ Z\ C\ I\ D\ V$$
$$/\ /\ /\ -\ -\ -$$

Addressing mode	Assembly language form		OP Code	No. Bytes	No. Cycles
Accumulator	ASL	A	0A	1	2
Zero Page	ASL	Oper	06	2	5
Zero Page, X	ASL	Oper, X	16	2	6
Absolute	ASL	Oper	0E	3	6
Absolute, X	ASL	Oper, X	1E	3	7

BCC
Branch on Carry Clear
Operation: Branch on C=0

$$N\ Z\ C\ I\ D\ V$$
$$-\ -\ -\ -\ -\ -$$

Addressing mode	Assembly language form		OP Code	No. Bytes	No. Cycles
Relative	BCC	Oper	90	2	2*

* Add 1 if branch occurs to same page.
* Add 2 if branch occurs to different page.

Branch on carry set
BCS
Operation: Branch on C=1

$$N\ Z\ C\ I\ D\ V$$
$$-\ -\ -\ -\ -\ -$$

Addressing mode	Assembly language form		OP Code	No. Bytes	No. Cycles
Relative	BCS	Oper	B0	2	2*

* Add 1 if branch occurs to same page.
* Add 2 if branch occurs to next page.

Branch on result zero
BEQ
Operation: Branch on Z=1

$$N\ Z\ C\ I\ D\ V$$
$$-\ -\ -\ -\ -\ -$$

Addressing mode	Assembly language form		OP Code	No. Bytes	No. Cycles
Relative	BEQ	Oper	F0	2	2*

* Add 1 if branch occurs to same page.
* Add 2 if branch occurs to next page.

BIT
Test bits in memory with accumulator

Operation: a∧M, M_7—N, M_6—V

N Z C I D V
M_7 / – – –M_6

Addressing mode	Assembly language form		OP Code	No. Bytes	No. Cycles
Zero Page	BIT	Oper	24	2	3
Absolute	BIT	Oper	2C	3	4

BMI
Branch on result minus

Operation: Branch on N=1

N Z C I D V
– – – – – –

Addressing mode	Assembly language form		OP Code	No. Bytes	No. Cycles
Relative	BMI	Oper	3Ø	2	2*

* Add 1 if branch occurs to same page.
* Add 2 if branch occurs to different page.

Branch on result not zero

BNE

Operation: Branch on Z=O

N Z C I D V
– – – – – –

Addressing mode	Assembly language form		OP Code	No. Bytes	No. Cycles
Relative	BNE	Oper	DØ	2	2*

* Add 1 if branch occurs to same page.
* Add 2 if branch occurs to different page.

Branch on result plus

BPL

Operation: Branch on N=Ø

N Z C I D V
– – – – – –

Addressing mode	Assembly language form		OP Code	No. Bytes	No. Cycles
Relative	BPL	Oper	1Ø	2	2*

* Add 1 if branch occurs to same page.
* Add 2 if branch occurs to different page.

BRK

Force Break

Operation: Forced Interrupt PC+2|P|

N Z C I D V
– – – * – –

Addressing mode	Assembly language form	OP Code	No. Bytes	No. Cycles
Implied	BRK	ØØ	1	7

* A BRK command cannot be masked by setting I.

BVC

Branch on overflow clear

Operation: Branch on V=O

N Z C I D V
– – – – – –

Addressing mode	Assembly language form	OP Code	No. Bytes	No. Cycles
Relative	BVC Oper	5Ø	2	2*

* Add 1 if branch occurs to same page.
* Add 2 if branch occurs to different page.

Branch on overflow set

BVS

Operation: Branch on V=1

N Z C I D V
– – – – – –

Addressing mode	Assembly language form	OP Code	No. Bytes	No. Cycles
Relative	BVS Oper	7Ø	2	2*

* Add 1 if branch occurs to same page.
* Add 2 if branch occurs to different page.

Clear carry flag

CLC

Operation: Ø—C

N Z C I D V
– – Ø – – –

Addressing mode	Assembly language form	OP Code	No. Bytes	No. Cycles
Implied	CLC	18	1	2

CLD

Clear decimal mode

Operation: Ø—D

N Z C I D V
– – – – Ø –

Addressing mode	Assembly language form	OP Code	No. Bytes	No. Cycles
Implied	CLD	D8	1	2

CLI

Clear interrupt disable bit

Operation: Ø—I

```
NZCIDV
- - - Ø - -
```

Addressing mode	Assembly language form	OP Code	No. Bytes	No. Cycles
Implied	CLI	58	1	2

CPX

Compare memory and index X

Operation: X—M

```
NZCIDV
/ / / - - -
```

Addressing mode	Assembly language form		OP Code	No. Bytes	No. Cycles
Immediate	CPX	#Oper	EØ	2	2
Zero Page	CPX	Oper	E4	2	3
Absolute	CPX	Oper	EC	3	4

CPY

Compare memory and index Y

Operation: Y—M

```
NZCIDV
/ / / - - -
```

Addressing mode	Assembly language form		OP Code	No. Bytes	No. Cycles
Immediate	CPY	#Oper	CØ	2	2
Zero Page	CPY	Oper	C4	2	3
Absolute	CPY	Oper	CC	3	4

Clear overflow flag

CLV

Operation: Ø—V

```
NZCIDV
- - - - - Ø
```

Addressing mode	Assembly language form	OP Code	No. Bytes	No. Cycles
Implied	CLV	B8	1	2

152

CMP

Compare memory and accumulator

Operation: A—M

N Z C I D V
/ / / – – –

Addressing mode	Assembly language form		OP Code	No. Bytes	No. Cycles
Immediate	CMP	#Oper	C9	2	2
Zero Page	CMP	Oper	C5	2	3
Zero Page, X	CMP	Oper, X	D5	2	4
Absolute	CMP	Oper	CD	3	4
Absolute, X	CMP	Oper, X	DD	3	4*
Absolute, Y	CMP	Oper, Y	D9	3	4*
(Indirect, X)	CMP	(Oper, X)	C1	2	6
(Indirect), Y	CMP	(Oper), Y	D1	2	5*

* Add 1 if page boundary is crossed.

DEC

Decrement memory by one

Operation: M-1—M

N Z C I D V
/ / – – – –

Addressing mode	Assembly language form		OP Code	No. Bytes	No. Cycles
Zero Page	DEC	Oper	C6	2	5
Zero Page, X	DEC	Oper, X	D6	2	6
Absolute	DEC	Oper	CE	3	6
Absolute, X	DEC	Oper, X	DE	3	7

DEX

Decrement index X by one

Operation: X-1X

N Z C I D V
/ / – – – –

Addressing mode	Assembly language form	OP Code	No. Bytes	No. Cycles
Implied	DEX	CA	1	2

DEY

Decrement index Y by one

Operation: Y-1—Y

N Z C I D V
/ / – – – –

Addressing mode	Assembly language form	OP Code	No. Bytes	No. Cycles
Implied	DEY	88	1	2

153

EOR
Exclusive—Or memory with accumulator

Operation: A-M—A

N Z C I D V
/ / — — — —

Addressing mode	Assembly language form		OP Code	No. Bytes	No. Cycles
Immediate	EOR	#Oper	49	2	2
Zero Page	EOR	Oper	45	2	3
Zero Page, X	EOR	Oper, X	55	2	4
Absolute	EOR	Oper	4D	3	4
Absolute, X	EOR	Oper, X	5D	3	4*
Absolute, Y	EOR	Oper, Y	59	3	4*
(Indirect, X)	EOR	(Oper, X)	41	2	6
(Indirect), Y	EOR	(Oper), Y	51	2	5*

* Add 1 if page boundary is crossed.

Increment memory by one

INC

Operation: M+1—M

N Z C I D V
/ / — — — —

Addressing mode	Assembly language form		OP Code	No. Bytes	No. Cycles
Zero Page	INC	Oper	E6	2	5
Zero Page, X	INC	Oper, X	F6	2	6
Absolute	INC	Oper	EE	3	6
Absolute, X	INC	Oper, X	FE	3	7

Increment index X by one

INX

Operation: X+1—X

N Z C I D V
/ / — — — —

Addressing mode	Assembly language form	OP Code	No. Bytes	No. Cycles
Implied	INX	E8	1	2

INY
Increment index Y by one

Operation: Y+1—Y

N Z C I D V
/ / — — — —

Addressing mode	Assembly language form	OP Code	No. Bytes	No. Cycles
Implied	INY	C8	1	2

154

JMP

Jump to new location

Operation: (PC+1)—PCL
(PC+2)—PCH

N Z C I D V
– – – – – –

Addressing mode	Assembly language form		OP Code	No. Bytes	No. Cycles
Absolute	JMP	Oper	4C	3	3
Indirect	JMP	(Oper)	6C	3	5

Jump to new location saving return address

JSR

Operation: PC+2|, (PC+1)—PCL
(PC+2)—PCH

N Z C I D V
– – – – – –

Addressing mode	Assembly language form		OP Code	No. Bytes	No. Cycles
Absolute	JSR	Oper	2Ø	3	6

Load accumulator with memory

LDA

Operation: M—A

N Z C I D V
/ / – – – –

Addressing mode	Assembly language form		OP Code	No. Bytes	No. Cycles
Immediate	LDA	#Oper	A9	2	2
Zero Page	LDA	Oper	A5	2	3
Zero Page, X	LDA	Oper, X	B5	2	4
Absolute	LDA	Oper	AD	3	4
Absolute, X	LDA	Oper, X	BD	3	4*
Absolute, Y	LDA	Oper, Y	B9	3	4*
(Indirect, X)	LDA	(Oper, X)	A1	2	6
(Indirect), Y	LDA	(Oper), Y	B1	2	5*

* Add 1 if page boundary is crossed.

LDX

Load index X with memory

Operation: M—X

N Z C I D V
/ / – – – –

Addressing mode	Assembly language form		OP Code	No. Bytes	No. Cycles
Immediate	LDX	#Oper	A2	2	2
Zero Page	LDX	Oper	A6	2	3
Zero Page, Y	LDX	Oper, Y	B6	2	4
Absolute	LDX	Oper	AE	3	4
Absolute, Y	LDX	Oper, Y	BE	3	4*

* Add 1 when page boundary is crossed.

155

LDY

Load index Y with memory

Operation: M—Y

N Z C I D V
/ / – – – –

Addressing mode	Assembly language form		OP Code	No. Bytes	No. Cycles
Immediate	LDY	#Oper	AØ	2	2
Zero Page	LDY	Oper	A4	2	3
Zero Page, X	LDY	Oper, X	B4	2	4
Absolute	LDY	Oper	AC	3	4
Absolute, X	LDY	Oper, X	BC	3	4*

* Add 1 when page boundary is crossed.

ORA

OR memory with accumulator

Operation: AVM—A

N Z C I D V
/ / – – – –

Addressing mode	Assembly language form		OP Code	No. Bytes	No. Cycles
Immediate	ORA	#Oper	Ø9	2	2
Zero Page	ORA	Oper	Ø5	2	3
Zero Page, X	ORA	Oper, X	15	2	4
Absolute	ORA	Oper	ØD	3	4
Absoulte, X	ORA	Oper, X	1D	3	4*
Absolute, Y	ORA	Oper, Y	19	3	4*
(Indirect, X)	ORA	(Oper, X)	Ø1	2	6
(Indirect), Y	ORA	(Oper), Y	11	2	5*

* Add 1 on page crossing.

PHA

Push accumulator on stack

Operation: A|

N Z C I D V
– – – – – –

Addressing mode	Assembly language form	OP Code	No. Bytes	No. Cycles
Implied	PHA	48	1	3

Shift right one bit (memory or accumulator)

LSR

Operation: Ø—7 6 5 4 3 2 1 Ø—C

N Z C I D V
Ø / / – – –

Addressing mode	Assembly language form		OP Code	No. Bytes	No. Cycles
Accumulator	LSR	A	4A	1	2
Zero Page	LSR	Oper	46	2	5
Zero Page, X	LSR	Oper, X	56	2	6
Absolute	LSR	Oper	4E	3	6
Absolute, X	LSR	Oper, X	5E	3	7

156

NOP

No operation

Operation: No operation (2 cycles)

N Z C I D V
_ _ _ _ _ _

Addressing mode	Assembly language form	OP Code	No. Bytes	No. Cycles
Implied	NOP	EA	1	2

PHP

Push processor status on stack

Operation: P|

N Z C I D V
_ _ _ _ _ _

Addressing mode	Assembly language form	OP Code	No. Bytes	No. Cycles
Implied	PHP	Ø8	1	3

PLA

Pull accumulator from stack

Operation: A|

N Z C I D V
/ / _ _ _ _

Addressing mode	Assembly language form	OP Code	No. Bytes	No. Cycles
Implied	PLA	68	1	4

PLP

Pull processor status from stack

Operation: P|

N Z C I D V
From Stack

Addressing mode	Assembly language form	OP Code	No. Bytes	No. Cycles
Implied	PLP	28	1	4

ROL

Rotate one bit left (memory or accumulator)

Operation: 7 6 5 4 3 2 1 Ø–C   [M or A]

N Z C I D V
/ / / _ _ _

Addressing mode	Assembly language form		OP Code	No. Bytes	No. Cycles
Accumulator	ROL	A	2A	1	2
Zero Page	ROL	Oper	26	2	5
Zero Page, X	ROL	Oper, X	36	2	6
Absolute	ROL	Oper	2E	3	6
Absolute, X	ROL	Oper, X	3E	3	7

157

ROR

Rotate one bit right (memory or accumulator)

```
             ┌─ M or A ─┐
Operation:  C—7 6 5 4 3 2 1 0
```

N Z C I D V
/ / / – – –

Addressing mode	Assembly language form		OP Code	No. Bytes	No. Cycles
Accumulator	ROR	A	6A	1	2
Zero Page	ROR	Oper	66	2	5
Zero Page, X	ROR	Oper, X	76	2	6
Absolute	ROR	Oper	6E	3	6
Absolute, X	ROR	Oper, X	7E	3	7

RTI

Return from interrupt

Operation: P | PC |

N Z C I D V
From Stack

Addressing mode	Assembly language form	OP Code	No. Bytes	No. Cycles
Implied	RTI	40	1	6

RTS

Return from subroutine

Operation: PC |, PC+1—PC

N Z C I D V
– – – – – –

Addressing mode	Assembly language form	OP Code	No. Bytes	No. Cycles
Implied	RTS	60	1	6

SBC

Subtract memory from accumulator with borrow

Operation: A−M−C̄—A
Note: C=Borrow

N Z C I D V
/ / / – – /

Addressing mode	Assembly language form		OP Code	No. Bytes	No. Cycles
Immediate	SBC	#Oper	E9	2	2
Zero Page	SBC	Oper	E5	2	3
Zero Page, X	SBC	Oper, X	F5	2	4
Absolute	SBC	Oper	ED	3	4
Absolute, X	SBC	Oper, X	FD	3	4*
Absolute, Y	SBC	Oper, Y	F9	3	4*
(Indirect, X)	SBC	(Oper, X)	E1	2	6
(Indirect), Y	SBC	(Oper), Y	F1	2	5*

* Add 1 when page boundary is crossed.

Set carry flag   **SEC**

Operation: 1—C

N Z C I D V
  – – 1 – – –

Addressing mode	Assembly language form	OP Code	No. Bytes	No. Cycles
Implied	SEC	38	1	2

Set decimal mode   **SED**

Operation: 1—D

N Z C I D V
  – – – – 1 –

Addressing mode	Assembly language form	OP Code	No. Bytes	No. Cycles
Implied	SED	F8	1	2

Set interrupt disable status   **SEI**

Operation: 1—I

N Z C I D V
  – – – 1 – –

Addressing mode	Assembly language form	OP Code	No. Bytes	No. Cycles
Implied	SEI	78	1	2

STA

Operation: A—M   Store accumulator in memory

N Z C I D V
  – – – – – –

Addressing mode	Assembly language form		OP Code	No. Bytes	No. Cycles
Zero Page	STA	Oper	85	2	3
Zero Page, X	STA	Oper, X	95	2	4
Absolute	STA	Oper	8D	3	4
Absolute, X	STA	Oper, X	9D	3	5
Absolute, Y	STA	Oper, Y	99	3	5
(Indirect, X)	STA	(Oper, X)	81	2	6
(Indirect), Y	STA	(Oper), Y	91	2	6

159

STX

Operation: X—M

Store index X in memory

N Z C I D V
- - - - - -

Addressing mode	Assembly language form		OP Code	No. Bytes	No. Cycles
Zero Page	STX	Oper	86	2	3
Zero Page, Y	STX	Oper, Y	96	2	4
Absolute	STX	Oper	8E	3	4

Store index Y in memory

STY

Operation: Y—M

N Z C I D V
- - - - - -

Addressing mode	Assembly language form		OP Code	No. Bytes	No. Cycles
Zero Page	STY	Oper	84	2	3
Zero Page, X	STY	Oper, X	94	2	4
Absolute	STY	Oper	8C	3	4

Transfer accumulator to index X

TAX

Operation: A—X

N Z C I D V
/ / - - - -

Addressing mode	Assembly language form	OP Code	No. Bytes	No. Cycles
Implied	TAX	AA	1	2

TAY

Operation: A—Y

Transfer accumulator to index Y

N Z C I D V
/ / - - - -

Addressing mode	Assembly language form	OP Code	No. Bytes	No. Cycles
Implied	TAY	A8	1	2

TYA

Operation: Y—A

Transfer index Y to accumulator

N Z C I D V
/ / - - - -

Addressing mode	Assembly language form	OP Code	No. Bytes	No. Cycles
Implied	TYA	98	1	2

160

Operation: S—X	Transfer stack pointer to index X		**TSX**
			N Z C I D V
			/ / − − − −

Addressing mode	Assembly language form	OP Code	No. Bytes	No. Cycles
Implied	TSX	BA	1	2

Operation: X—A	Transfer index X to accumulator		**TXA**
			N Z C I D V
			/ / − − − −

Addressing mode	Assembly language form	OP Code	No. Bytes	No. Cycles
Implied	TXA	8A	1	2

Operation: X—S	Transfer index X to stack pointer		**TXS**
			N Z C I D V
			− − − − − −

Addressing mode	Assembly language form	OP Code	No. Bytes	No. Cycles
Implied	TXS	9A	1	2

ØØ –BRK
Ø1 –ORA—(Indirect, X)
Ø2 –Future Expansion
Ø3 –Future Expansion
Ø4 –Future Expansion
Ø5 –ORA—Zero Page
Ø6 –ASL—Zero Page
Ø7 –Future Expansion
Ø8 –PHP
Ø9 –ORA—Immediate
ØA –ASL—Accumulator
ØB –Future Expansion
ØC –Future Expansion
ØD –ORA—Absolute
ØE –ASL—Absolute
ØF –Future Expansion
1Ø –BPL
11 –ORA—(Indirect), Y
12 –Future Expansion
13 –Future Expansion
14 –Future Expansion
15 –ORA—Zero Page, X
16 –ASL—Zero Page, X
17 –Future Expansion
18 –CLC
19 –ORA—Absolute, Y
1A –Future Expansion
1B –Future Expansion
1C –Future Expansion
1D –ORA—Absolute, X
1E –ASL—Absolute, X
1F –Future Expansion
2Ø –JSR
21 –AND—(Indirect, X)
22 –Future Expansion
23 –Future Expansion
24 –BIT—Zero Page
25 –AND—Zero Page

26	–ROL—Zero Page	52	–Future Expansion
27	–Future Expansion	53	–Future Expansion
28	–PLP	54	–Future Expansion
29	–AND—Immediate	55	–EOR—Zero Page, X
2A	–ROL—Accumulator	56	–LSR—Zero Page, X
2B	–Future Expansion	57	–Future Expansion
2C	–BIT—Absolute	58	–CLI
2D	–AND—Absolute	59	–EOR—Absolute, Y
2E	–ROL—Absolute	5A	–Future Expansion
2F	–Future Expansion	5B	–Future Expansion
3Ø	–BMI	5C	–Future Expansion
31	–AND—(Indirect), Y	5D	–EOR—Absolute, X
32	–Future Expansion	5E	–LSR—Absolute, X
33	–Future Expansion	5F	–Future Expansion
34	–Future Expansion	6Ø	–RTS
35	–AND—Zero Page, X	61	–ADC—(Indirect, X)
36	–ROL—Zero Page, X	62	–Future Expansion
37	–Future Expansion	63	–Future Expansion
38	–SEC	64	–Future Expansion
39	–AND—Absolute, Y	65	–ADC—Zero Page
3A	–Future Expansion	66	–ROR—Zero Page
3B	–Future Expansion	67	–Future Expansion
3C	–Future Expansion	68	–PLA
3D	–AND—Absolute, X	69	–ADC—Immediate
3E	–ROL—Absolute, X	6A	–ROR—Accumulator
3F	–Future Expansion	6B	–Future Expansion
4Ø	–RTI	6C	–JMP—Indirect
41	–EOR—(Indirect, X)	6D	–ADC—Absolute
42	–Future Expansion	6E	–ROR—Absolute
43	–Future Expansion	6F	–Future Expansion
44	–Future Expansion	7Ø	–BVS
45	–EOR—Zero Page	71	–ADC—(Indirect), Y
46	–LSR—Zero Page	72	–Future Expansion
47	–Future Expansion	73	–Future Expansion
48	–PHA	74	–Future Expansion
49	–EOR—Immediate	75	–ADC—Zero Page, X
4A	–LSR—Accumulator	76	–ROR—Zero Page, X
4B	–Future Expansion	77	–Future Expansion
4C	–JMP—Absolute	78	–SEI
4D	–EOR—Absolute	79	–ADC—Absolute, Y
4E	–LSR—Absolute	7A	–Future Expansion
4F	–Future Expansion	7B	–Future Expansion
5Ø	–BVC	7C	–Future Expansion
51	–EOR—(Indirect), Y	7D	–ADC—Absolute, X

7E –ROR—Absolute, X	AA–TAX
7F –Future Expansion	AB –Future Expansion
8Ø –Future Expansion	AC–LDY—Absolute
81 –STA—(Indirect, X)	AD–LDA—Absolute
82 –Future Expansion	AE–LDX—Absolute
83 –Future Expansion	AF –Future Expansion
84 –STY—Zero Page	BØ –BCS
85 –STA—Zero Page	B1 –LDA—(Indirect), Y
86 –STX—Zero Page	B2 –Future Expansion
87 –Future Expansion	B3 –Future Expansion
88 –DEY	B4 –LDT—Zero Page, X
89 –Future Expansion	B5 –LDA—Zero Page, X
8A –TXA	B6 –LDX—Zero Page, Y
8B –Future Expansion	B7 –Future Expansion
8C –STY—Absolute	B8 –CLV
8D –STA—Absolute	B9 –LDA—Absolute, Y
8E –STX—Absolute	BA–TSX
8F –Future Expansion	BB –Future Expansion
9Ø –BCC	BC–LDY—Absolute, X
91 –STA—(Indirect), Y	BD–LDA—Absolute, X
92 –Future Expansion	BE–LDX—Absolute, Y
93 –Future Expansion	BF –Future Expansion
94 –STY—Zero Page, X	CØ –CPY—Immediate
95 –STA—Zero Page, X	C1 –CMP—(Indirect, X)
96 –STX—Zero Page, Y	C2 –Future Expansion
97 –Future Expansion	C3 –Future Expansion
98 –TYA	C4 –CPY—Zero Page
99 –STA—Absolute, Y	C5 –CMP—Zero Page
9A –TXS	C6 –DEC—Zero Page
9B –Future Expansion	C7 –Future Expansion
9C –Future Expansion	C8 –INY
9D –STA—Absolute, X	C9 –CMP—Immediate
9E –Future Expansion	CA–DEX
9F –Future Expansion	CB –Future Expansion
AØ –LDY—Immediate	CC–CPY—Absolute
A1 –LDA—(Indirect, X)	CD–CMP—Absolute
A2 –LDX—Immediate	CE–DEC—Absolute
A3 –Future Expansion	CF –Future Expansion
A4 –LDY—Zero Page	DØ –BNE
A5 –LDA—Zero Page	D1 –CMP—(Indirect), Y
A6 –LDX—Zero Page	D2 –Future Expansion
A7 –Future Expansion	D3 –Future Expansion
A8 –TAY	D4 –Future Expansion
A9 –LDA—Immediate	D5 –CMP—Zero Page, X

D6 –DEC—Zero Page, X
D7 –Future Expansion
D8 –CLD
D9 –CMP—Absolute, Y
DA–Future Expansion
DB–Future Expansion
DC–Future Expansion
DD–CMP—Absolute, X
DE–DEC—Absolute, X
DF–Future Expansion
E0 –CPX—Immediate
E1 –SBC—(Indirect, X)
E2 –Future Expansion
E3 –Future Expansion
E4 –CPX—Zero Page
E5 –SBC—Zero Page
E6 –INC—Zero Page
E7 –Future Expansion
E8 –INX
E9 –SBC—Immediate
EA–NOP

EB –Future Expansion
EC –CPX—Absolute
ED–SBC—Absolute
EE –INC—Absolute
EF –Future Expansion
F0 –BEQ
F1 –SBC—(Indirect), Y
F2 –Future Expansion
F3 –Future Expansion
F4 –Future Expansion
F5 –SBC—Zero Page, X
F6 –INC—Zero Page, X
F7 –Future Expansion
F8 –SED
F9 –SBC—Absolute, Y
FA–Future Expansion
FB –Future Expansion
FC –Future Expansion
FD–SBC—Absolute, X
FE –INC—Absolute, X
FF –Future Expansion

Index

165